THE SOUTH CAROLINA
CIVIL WAR OF 1775

Other Books by Lewis Pinckney Jones:

BOOKS AND ARTICLES ON
SOUTH CAROLINA HISTORY
A List for Laymen (1970)

SOUTH CAROLINA
A Synoptic History for Laymen (1971)

STORMY PETREL
N. G. Gonzales and His State (1973)

THE SOUTH CAROLINA CIVIL WAR OF 1775

by

LEWIS PINCKNEY JONES

South Carolina History Illustrated
Pamphlet Series Number 1

THE SANDLAPPER STORE, INC.

Library of Congress Catalog Card Number: 75-32396
International Standard Book Number: 0-87844-027-5
Manufactured in the United States of America

To a wife, Denny, who continues to have the patience that permits one to pursue such rivals as "Tories" and "Whigs."

To a master teacher, Fletcher M. Green, whose influence and inspiration last so long on so many.

Contents

Introduction

In some respects the terms or phrases frequently used to describe world conditions of 1945 to 1975 seem eerily descriptive of the conditions and tensions which marked the province of South Carolina during the year 1775. There was a tense "cold war" between two factions, both of whom were sincerely devoted to contrasting and competing principles and political philosophies. In general, these factions inhabited different areas. Both talked much of "freedom" and "liberty," but the words meant different things to each faction. Both thundered mightily about their concern for a "constitution" and yet certainly they did not have the same ideas about what was "constitutional." Both groups were made up of sincere "patriots" but suspected that the other was composed of "traitors." Some impetuous souls advocated "brinkmanship" and occasionally were tempted to "pre-emptive strikes" or to "preventive war." There was enough cruelty and harshness that at times one senses the marks of a "reign of terror." Amid groups of sincere men and statesmen were also some venal souls and also some who picked sides simply because of their own vested or personal interests.

By the end of the year, after much marching and counter-marching, a somewhat uneasy peace or "detente" had been achieved after some "summit meetings." The "detente" was sufficiently secure that the more radical faction could now turn their backs on those who had embraced "neutralism" and concentrate their efforts on the struggle with Great Britain — a struggle which was not new but which was to reach a desperate stage in 1776.

ix

Chapter One
Plutocrats Who Were Radicals

Once Julius Caesar had crossed the Rubicon in 49 B. C. in his bid to return to Italy and launch a *coup d'etat* for government change, the die was definitely cast and events moved swiftly. The year 1775 was occasion for the English colonists of South Carolina also to cross a Rubicon, but instead of a swift passage the commonwealth floundered adrift all year in its Rubicon until finally one group of tugging leaders seemed to have nudged the colony off on a radical course. There were to be waverings and shifts of course thereafter, but by year's end one faction appeared to be in firm control after a dramatic and tumultuous year.

Throughout the preceding decade, the coastal part of South Carolina had been gripped by a complex and involved wrangle with the mother country. There had been much talk of the English constitution, the "rights of Englishmen," a Stamp Act, "taxation without representation," the Townshend Acts, tea parties and other nuisances and controversies. In addition, South Carolina devised some special controversies of its own with England — the Wilkes Fund case, and the issue of whether or not the Governor's Council of the colony was or was not an upper house of its Parliament.[1]

Neither revolution nor secession, however, seemed a likely prospect when 1775 dawned. Nor was either inevitable. True, the First Continental Congress had already met in Philadelphia in the fall of 1774 and included South Carolinians chosen by what amounted to "pick-up committees" of dissidents. These South Carolina spokesmen were to join in summarizing continent-wide grievances which charged that Westminster allegedly was making policy changes in defiance of the unwritten English constitution.

The South Carolina protest movement took on new formality and the semblance of government (albeit extra-legal and in defiance of the established government) with the first meeting of the Provincial Congress in the Exchange Building in Charlestown on January 11, 1775. Such replaced the earlier "general meetings" and self-appointed groups that had been speaking for discontented South Carolinians.[2] Now the Congress gave semblance of dignity and the appearances of speaking for the local "power structure."

The Provincial Congress did "look like a government" in action since the British colonial legislature (Commons House of Assembly) was virtually in limbo, having been prorogued by royal governors because of impasses connected with the Wilkes Fund.[3] Actually many members of the Provincial Congress were the self-same leaders of the Carolina coastal plutocracy who also held seats in the moribund Assembly.

Up to this point, those Carolinians who chose the "radical" course of strong protests and harsh debate were hardly "radical" in the twentieth-century connotation — which holds such figures as Trotsky, Lenin or Mussolini as stereotypes for "radicals." By and large, those radicals were "gentlemen" — with names like Laurens, Middleton, Pinckney or Rutledge — the long-respected leadership whose role was rarely questioned too impolitely by those of lesser social and economic standing. They were the men of affairs (personally or directly) affected by a Stamp Act, by trade restrictions or by suppression of the Commons House of Assembly, a body which was not exactly "common." The term "radical" in the South Carolina controversy should not necessarily evoke pictures of mobs in the streets, armed brawls or even insults to British flags. Impelled by differing motives, some selfish and some not, within the colony there was emerging "revolution from above," sponsored by the privileged groups who were divided on how strong a protest to make but who were generally agreed on obtaining somehow a restoration of their constitutional liberties,[4] and who were certainly determined that they were *not* seeking a revolution that would turn society wrong side out.

The election for the First Provincial Congress that convened early in 1775 tells much about South Carolina attitudes and portended some of the reason for disunity as the colony confronted mother country "iniquity" later that year. The Assembly — the official British legislature for the colony — had never been democratic nor representative, but reflected primarily the propertied gentlemen

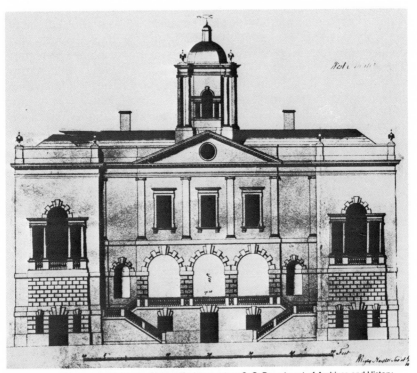

Photo reproduction by Richard Taylor, courtesy S. C. Department of Archives and History

The Exchange Building was the site where the Revolutionary bodies first began their efforts to organize the province in its resistance to the royal ministry. The roof and entranceway of the present structure vary somewhat from this architect's drawing, dated 1766.

along the coast where Anglican Church parishes served as precincts. Long had the Back Country cried foul — especially since 1750 when it had begun rapidly filling up with not particularly genteel newcomers who had neither voice in nor service from their colonial government.[5] The General Committee that arranged for the election of the Provincial Congress now threw a crumb to the settlers on the frontier, that is, roughly all the area more than sixty miles from salt water: The town (nobody needed to name it) was allotted thirty seats; the parishes were allotted six each; and the Back Country was divided into four large districts with ten members each. The result: The Back Country had only forty of one hundred eighty-four representatives, yet it had three-fourths of the population.[6] This was a step forward in that they had had none before[7], but it was hardly likely to transform them into an appreciative and enthusiastic cheering section for the ruling Low Country oligarchy in the latter's long-simmering row with England — a row which had neither concerned the Piedmont settlers nor threatened their way of life or liberty. As Historian Edward McCrady pointed out, it is not known whether the people in general took part in this election conducted in late 1774 by "influential gentlemen in every parish and district" who "took care, no doubt, to see that only those were returned who were favorable to the cause."[8] Another South Carolina historian, David Duncan Wallace, noted that "the assemblage was revolutionary, and the means of selecting it were, as usual in revolutions, such as to secure the ascendancy of the moving party."[9] Even where "the bipeds of the forest" did participate, they chose some scions of the Low Country to the Provincial Congress. Edward Rutledge, for example, was chosen in Ninety Six and Henry Middleton in the area between the Broad and Catawba rivers. Certainly they were hardly frontiersmen in coonskins.

Ironic was the relation of this radical body to the chief official of England resident in the colony. For decades, the mother country had been sending over native Britons as governors, a practice which perhaps avoided divided loyalty but also sometimes promoted poor judgment or insensitivity. The lieutenant-governor, however, was usually a native Carolinian. His position was not "a heartbeat away from the governorship," providing a standby in case of gubernatorial death. Instead, during the intervals when there was no royal governor present in the colony (such intervals were fairly frequent and sometimes prolonged) the lieutenant-governor served as acting chief executive. In the first half of 1775 such a situation

EDWARD RUTLIDGE

Edward Rutledge

Lithograph by Ole Erekson, 1876

Edward Rutledge (1749-1800) was a signer of the Declaration of Independence and a governor. Although a lawyer of the Low Country aristocracy, he was elected to the First Provincial Congress by the Ninety Six area. He was a brother of John Rutledge, who was also a governor.

prevailed, and the position of lieutenant-governor was filled by William Bull, a native of Charlestown and member of a prominent family at Ashley Hall plantation. (Earlier, his father of the same name had also held the position.)

South Carolina has had no more eminent citizen nor statesmanlike governor than this William Bull. "As Speaker of the Commons, member of the Council, General of Militia, and Lieutenant Governor, he had been in the public service for thirty-five years."[10] He had served nine years as acting chief executive. He was loyal to the King and constitution, and faithful to the stewardship which he had accepted with his office. He was also friend and neighbor of now-tumultuous Carolinians, who in their tumult never wavered in treating both Bull and his office with respect, decorum and tact so long as he held it. Several prominent scholars have noted that had the mother country given him the governor's post, full confidence and greater freedom of action, he "might possibly have successfully resisted the revolutionary movements in South Carolina," so held in respect was he.[11] One might even wonder if some sort of British dominion status might not have been successful if England had had a supply of William Bulls for governorships — and the willingness to delegate authority to them.

In its first month, the First Provincial Congress sent an address "to the Honorable William Bull, Esquire": "We his Majesty's faithful and loyal subjects, the Representatives of all the good people in this Colony, now met in provincial Congress, think ourselves indispensably obliged to address your Honour, for redress of a grievance, which threatens destruction to the constitution, and ruin...." The grievance: the continued "disuse of General Assemblies." The address was phrased in formal and respectful phrases, and received a reply couched in similar terms from Bull to the "gentlemen of respectable characters and property in this province," who were assured by the Lieutenant-Governor that he would "under the guidance of my duty to the King and zeal for the service of the province, do every thing in my power, that can contribute to the public welfare."[12]

Despite dignity and decorum, the Congress that same day resolved that all inhabitants "be diligently attentive in learning the use of arms," and also set aside February 17 "as a day of fasting, humiliation and prayer, before Almighty God, devoutly to petition him to inspire the King with true wisdom, to defend the people of North America in their just title to freedom, and to avert from them the impending calamities of civil war."[13] There is no record as to what William Bull was praying in his house a few streets away. On the designated day, carrying the historic mace of the Commons House with them, the pious Provincial Congress went in procession to St. Philip's Church to hear a sermon directed by their orders to be "suitable to the importance of the occasion." Preachers presumably received inspiration from somewhere other than on high.

The Congress also reelected the five delegates to the next meeting of the Continental Congress slated for May to act with other colonies on measures "necessary for the recovery and establement of American rights and liberties, and for restoring harmony between Great Britain and her colonies."[14]

Although the Provincial Congress did not meet from January to June, its General Committee continued to exist and foment restlessness, and the vehicle of radicalism was accelerated by an aristocratic firebrand, young William Henry Drayton, whose home was the imposing Drayton Hall plantation on the Ashley. More impetuous than the moderate Henry Laurens, and much more radical than the conservative Rawlins Lowndes, the colorful Drayton cannot be depicted or judged with accuracy.[15] Like so many leaders of this era, Drayton was not permanently on one side of the issue: In the 1760s he had strongly defended the royal position and bitterly opposed non-importation tactics of economic warfare and pressure. As Robert Weir observed, his conversion "to one of the most demagogic leaders of the Revolution is puzzling." Aristocratic and ambitious, he early developed antipathy to placemen (political hacks sent to fill government posts in the colonies). Weir suggests that he perhaps became disillusioned with the English when he was not properly appreciated and treated with deference in the mother country where he lived temporarily (1769-72) after his support of the King. On the other hand, his swings in position could have been sincere and philosophically consistent; after all, when writing pamphlets first opposing stubborn colonists and later stubborn ministries, he signed both with the same pen name: *Freeman*. In any case, as Weir notes, "Like many converts, he became a zealous champion of the new cause."[16]

Rash propagandist that he was, Drayton was not unwise enough to propose yet secession among a people "still loyal to old England, regarding all their troubles as owing to a wicked ministry, resistance to which on their part in America would enable their friends, the Whigs, at home to overthrow."[17] As McCrady well put it, if Drayton this early had advocated independence, "he would have been more than a rebel — he would have been a traitor...."[18]

Here he served briefly as a circuit judge in 1774 and turned his charges to Back Country juries into flaming stump speeches attacking English policy and embracing the defiant rebels.[19] He was also a member of the Council, but at the request of other members of that body (a once-prestigious body now dominated by detested placemen), he was removed from it by Governor William Bull, his uncle, in March 1775, his fellow Councilors having charged him with seeking "to subvert the Constitution and unhinge government."[20]

Certainly Drayton's membership in the Council was anomalous, or at least inconsistent, since two months before his removal he had been appointed chairman of the radical Secret Committee of Five, a body which showed the extent to which radicalism was brewing. He was thus adroitly working both sides of the street, being member of a royal body and of a radical agency simultaneously. The Provincial Congress authorized his Secret Committee "to procure and distribute such articles, as the present state of the interior parts of this Colony renders necessary, for the better defense and security of the good people of thos parts, *and other necessary purposes*."[21] The sting was in the last four words, a blank check which could have spawned eighteenth-century vigilantes.[22] As February and March rolled into spring in 1775, it became obvious that America's "Whig friends" in Westminster were not disposed to divert policy to one more palatable for discontented colonists.

In the growing embroilment, the Secret Committee began to exercise its broad authority. On the night of April 21, this dedicated-but-decorous bunch relieved the English establishment of eight hundred guns, two hundred cutlasses and sixteen hundred pounds of powder from powder magazines and from the State House itself.[23] With the backing of the leading Charlestonians, the coup could have been conducted in broad open daylight, but as Drayton explained, they did it at night "as there was no reason for insulting the authority of the Lieutenant-Governor, who was much respected and beloved...."[24] Equally decorous correspondence ensued as face was saved all around: Governor Bull dutifully reported the shocking loss to the Commons House, where most of the perpetrators of the deed sat (as he very well knew); with furrowed brows they studied the mystery and later reported quite formally to His Excellency that they had been unable to solve the case of the missing arms but had "reasons to suppose that some of the inhabitants of this colony may have been induced to take so extraordinary and uncommon a step in consequence of the late alarming accounts from Great Britain."[25] Thus ended the minuet in ink, a farce which nevertheless showed how events were rolling downhill. D. D. Wallace stressed the import of the nocturnal break-in to seize arms: "The plan was executed which made the participants British traitors or American patriots according as the outcome should determine."[26] There is wise perception in Wallace's clear-cut evaluation — although a modern examining the dichotomy of treason or heroism may find it hard to imagine a later America devoid of the Order of the Cincinnati, the Sons of the American Revolution or the Daughters of the American Revolution!

The Secret Committee did not let the pot stop boiling that spring. To "throw odium on the British Administration" and "to invigorate the ardor of the people," this propaganda group devised a large "public exhibition" with effigies depicting the Pope, the Devil, Lord Grenville and Lord North. Like a float in a Mardi Gras parade, this "uncommon spectacle" was rolled into Broad Street adjacent to St. Michael's Church early in the morning. Whenever placemen or Crown officials passed by, the "Pope immediately bowed with proportioned respect to them" and the Devil aimed a dart at the head of the Pope.[27]

On May 3 the rebels' temperature went to fever readings with receipt of a letter from Arthur Lee, old confrere of John Wilkes and now confidential correspondent of the Continental Congress in London, charging that the British were planning to sponsor both a slave uprising and an Indian war against the colonists. No spectre was so calculated to spread terror to the Low Country white minority as the thought of slave rebellion, nor to the frontiersmen as the image of red savages on the warpath. As the Governor depicted the mood, "Words, I am told, cannot express the flame that this occasioned amongst all ranks and degrees; the cruelty and savage barbarity of the scheme was the conversation of all companies."[28] The fact that the rumor was false did not minimize the fact: Men act and react on the basis of what they believe to be true, whether it is or not. Their acceptance of the story is also evidence of how the agitated populace was disposed to believe the worst about British officialdom. This alarm over slave rebellions and Indian uprisings would recur — always with the same emotional effects.

On that same day (May 3), the South Carolina delegates sailed to Philadelphia for the second session of the Continental Congress, and within a week news of the Battle of Lexington arrived.[29] The General Committee promptly summoned the Provincial Congress to meet June 1 for its second session.[30] Col. Charles Pinckney, a "reluctant revolutionist,"[31] resigned the presidency and was replaced by Henry Laurens now that matters were reaching a crucial stage.

Pinckney's resignation underscored the fact that all members of the Congress were not of a single mind. A small, vigorous minority was willing to push boldly toward independence, seeing it as the inevitable outcome of the commotion. This faction centered around three firebrands: Christopher Gadsden, William Henry Drayton and Arthur Middleton. A larger group led by John Rutledge and Rawlins Lowndes might be depicted as rebels but not secessionists — willing to defend their rights by force of arms if necessary, determined on "Liberty under the crown." In between — but not vacillating — stood a man of moderation, one of the most distinguished men produced in South Carolina, Henry Laurens, new president of the Congress. In May, Alexander Innes, a prominent British official, probably depicted the mood of most of the radicals well when he observed that "the language of all is to have things restored to the situation they were in in 1763."[32]

The division in the Congress reflected attitudes of informed South Carolinians of the day. (Most of the "informed" ones lived in the Charlestown area where the colony's newspaper, the *South Carolina Gazette,* stridently opposed British policy.) No Gallup polls tell us with assurance public attitudes; but historians have long leaned on John Adams' observation that one-third of the Americans came to oppose independence, one-third favored it and the other third did not give a merry whoop. A recent appraisal by Eric F. Goldman suggested that just before the Revolutionary War half the colonists were indifferent to the whole clamor. Of the remaining half, he concluded that twenty percent were Loyalists and thirty percent were pro-independence.[33] In South Carolina, these last two figures might be reversed, and both certainly fluctuated considerably between 1775 and 1783 with many Carolinians changing their views and positions — some of them more than once.

Despite their differences, the Provincial Congress moved briskly and firmly during June 1775. If the analogy of the Rubicon crossing may be raised, it might be noted that the men in the pilot house of the ferry suddenly lurched ahead and seemed to be steaming steadily for

Charles Cotesworth Pinckney (1746-1825) was a member of the Council of Safety, served in the Revolutionary War and became a brigadier general in the Continental Army. In the 1790s he became a prominent diplomat.

the distant shore. (They were soon to learn, however, that all the passengers did not approve of the perhaps-perilous destination.)

On the second day of their session, it was "resolved *unanimously*, That a general ASSOCIATION is necessary,"[34] The General Committee had already secretly and heatedly debated the wisdom of demanding that inhabitants associate themselves with their neighbors in a solemn oath as commitment to active measures of hostility.[35] Now on June 3, the Congress called on citizens to pledge their lives and fortunes in defense of their liberties.

This statement of two hundred twelve words to which people were to be asked to pledge by signing was no mild, nebulous phrasing of empty platitudes.[36] Calling attention to military action in New England, the Association indicted "a wicked and despotic ministry" as being sufficient "to drive an oppressed people to the use of arms." Hence, in the stilted but formal language of the eighteenth century, the Congress called on subscribers to resist force with force, uniting against every foe, "Hereby solemnly engaging that, whenever our Continental or Provincial Councils shall decree it necessary, we will go forth, and be ready to sacrifice our lives and fortunes to secure her [South Carolina's] freedom and safety. This obligation [is] to continue in full force until a reconciliation shall take place between Great-Britain and America, upon constitutional principles — an Event which we most ardently desire." The Provincial Congress had reached a mood where it was going to ask Carolinians to fish or cut bait.

It was not a declaration of independence, but a declaration of war — and South Carolinians were now to be pressured to sign the Association. Moderate man that he was and interested in liberty of conscience for others as well as for himself, Henry Laurens strongly opposed the demand that non-signers be treated as public enemies.[37] Having stated his reservations, he and all the Congress signed, but the last sentence carried a threat: "And we will hold all those persons inimical to the liberty of the colonies, who shall refuse to subscribe this association." Soon "non-subscribers" were made amenable to the General Committee, and by them punishable "consistent to sound policy"[38] — an ill-defined, ominous guideline which could sanction duress, ostracism, vigilante activity, tar and feathers, and other attitudes hardly congenial with "liberty" or "constitutional Principles."[39]

One reading today the Journal of the Provincial Congress for June 1775 can sense the drama and rush of a nation suddenly, efficiently and inexorably mobilizing and girding for war. The responsibility and organization of the task was entrusted to the Council of Safety [40] consisting of thirteen men who were given considerable fiscal authority and virtual dictatorial powers over military recruitment. Three new regiments of militia were established by the Congress, joining twelve existing older Colonial regiments which might or might not prove loyal to the Congress. Acting with optimism, the Congress ordered militia colonels to hold one-third of the men in each company ready for instant service.[41]

However revolutionary its stance, the Provincial Congress was certainly no covert operation despite its decision that "the doors be kept shut during the present sitting of the Congress." Ironically, though, this revolutionary body met in the Assembly room of the State House itself.[42] When the new royal governor, Sir William Campbell, arrived on June 18 (and thus sent William Bull back into retirement),[43] the Congress sent him a formal and dignified "Address"[44] to "disclose to your Excellency the true cause of our present proceedings" so that the new official might "receive no unfavourable impression of our conduct, but that we may stand justified to the world." Although they noted that "the ordinary modes of application for redress of grievances" had failed, they alleged that it was "unnecessary to enumerate the grievances of America — they have been so often represented, that your Excellency cannot be a stranger to them." (They then proceeded to note a few of them again anyhow.) They gave George III personally some benefit of doubt, noting that "slanderous informations and wicked Counsels" had led him "into measures, which, if persisted in, must inevitably involve America in all the calamities of Civil War." As always, there was the olive branch as they besought the Governor to relay now the right word to their Sovereign, because "We only desire the secure employment of our invaluable rights; and we wish for nothing more ardently, than a speedy reconciliation with our mother-country, upon constitutional principles." These Congressmen, who considered themselves "his Majesty's loyal subjects," professed — good Whigs that they were — that they had "no desire of altering the Constitutuion...and no lust for independence," but did "readily profess our loyal attachment to our Sovereign, his Crown, and dignity; and trusting the event to Providence, we prefer death to slavery." They claimed to presume that Lord William would understand "that our taking up arms, is the result of dire necessity." In its tone and in its eloquence, the Carolina manifesto has some of

King George III reigned over Britain from 1760 to 1820. This engraving by Anthony Cardou was drawn by W. Hopkins from the original by Sir W. Beechy.

the ringing note in the more famous "Declaration of the Causes and Necessity of Taking Up Arms," drafted by John Dickinson and Thomas Jefferson and adopted by the Continental Congress two weeks later.[45]

Campbell, as Bull had done earlier, simply replied that he knew no representatives of the people except the Commons House of Assembly. Nevertheless, he pled that he was "incompetent to judge of the disputes which at present unhappily subsist," but assured the recalcitrant Congress that "no representation shall ever be made by me, but what shall be strictly consistent with truth, and with an earnest endeavour to promote the real happiness and prosperity of the province."[46]

The old bugaboos of Indian scalpings and slave uprisings acerbated Congress and the Council of Safety as the Charlestown summer warmed. The alleged conspirator was John Stuart, Superintendent of Indian Affairs, who resided in Charlestown.[47] But he had fled in May and by June 21 was in St. Augustine, which was under English control.[48] The report about Stuart came from a North Carolinian via Drayton to the secret Committee of Intelligence. On June 21, letters concerning Stuart were presented to the Congress which then ordered a letter sent to him about his "attempting to incite the Indians to hostilities."[49] His reply — dated July 18, St. Augustine — denied that he could or would "wantonly use any influence with Indians, to make them fall upon innocent people."[50] The Council of Safety went so far as to try, in effect, to bribe Alexander Cameron, Stuart's deputy among the Cherokees, to defect to their side. In this June fervor, the Secret Committee highjacked at the mouth of the Savannah a schooner carrying powder which was reputedly destined for the Indians.[51] Stuart had earlier written Lord Dartmouth[52] that propaganda about slave and Indian uprisings was simply agitation to justify arming the people and to get their support for the radical faction.[53] One cannot ignore, however, earlier friction between Stuart and Drayton when the Indian agent had stymied a remarkable plan of Drayton's for getting personal control of a huge tract of land occupied by the Catawba Indians along the river of that name. (Such personal vendettas, alas, often shape history — and even revolutions.)[54] Stuart had also been one of those instrumental in getting Drayton removed from the royal Council early in 1775.[55] It was not surprising then that in 1775 Stuart should blame his troubles on Drayton, "an unprincipled Villain who would Stick at nothing to gratify an unmanly revenge."[56]

The turmoil led Drayton to call on Mrs. Stuart at her home in Charlestown and force her to surrender letters from her husband. The same scene was repeated at the post office.[57] The extent of the vigilantism of the radicals — usually such formal and dignified gentlemen — is evident in the Congress' action the following winter when the gentlemen of that body resolved that "it is expedient and necessary, that the lady and daughter of John Stuart, Esq., be restrained from absenting themselves from his house in Charles-Town" and that "proper guards be immediately placed, and continued, about the house of the said John Stuart." At least, be it said to the credit of the courtly radicals that they did graciously designate two captains to "wait on Mrs. Stuart...and acquaint her of the order."[58] Thus, during a reign of terror the lady became a hostage for the "good conduct" of her husband, then a refugee in Florida.

The alarmed Congressmen themselves contributed to the restlessness of the Indians — especially the Cherokees — on the western border of the province by understandably being stingy with powder, arms and other goods which usually came to them from Charlestown. The Council of Safety also worried about the Catawbas (along the present North Carolina border) and had Drayton draft "a talk" to them. Samples:

> Brothers, we take you by the hand. The white people of this country, who live among you, desire that you will open your ears.... But if you do not mind what we say, you will be sorry for it by and by.
>
> The Great King, over the Great Water, has got some bad men about him, who every day give him a bad talk about us.... And they persuade the Great King to take our money out of our pockets, whether we will or not, which you know is a very bad thing.

If the Catawbas did not know it was "a very bad thing," they may have been convinced after several pages of such explanation. But they also got a severe warning of what dire things would happen to them if Charlestown should receive any "bad talk" about Catawbas' joining Cherokees in order "to set up the war-whoop this summer" since "we have now got a great many more warriors than we had last war." For the time, the "balance of terror" between whites and "the first Americans" was maintained in this early cold war.[59]

Equally explosive was the continuing rumor of slave uprisings in a colony where in 1775 there were 110,000 slaves (mostly concentrated in the tidewater area) and only 90,000 whites.[60] Perhaps Arthur Lee in London had originated the whole thing in his letter,[61] but it was easy for nervous South Carolinians to believe the worst. If anything was designed to galvanize the phobia-ridden Low Country aristocracy into a united, anti-British stance, this was it, for "of all human factors determining the nature of the Carolina Society, the silent influence of the black African was the most subtle, the most forceful, and most pervading, and the most lasting."[62] Drayton's Secret Committee was thus charged with providing plans to provide for "the security of the good people of this colony" and to set up patrols to watch for a slave revolt. In July, the Council of Safety took note of "the conduct of one John Burnett, holding nocturnal meetings with the negroes."[63] He was summoned before the Council and issued a warning to be more circumspect.[64] Some restlessness among a few blacks in Charlestown unleashed the terror which led to the hanging of one Jerry, a free Negro.[65]

Not surprisingly in the temper of such times, South Carolina in June witnessed its first examples of tarring and feathering — two victims that month and another in August. Henry Laurens, president of both the Congress and the Council, deprecated such excess which did their cause more harm than good.

In the Council of Safety's uncertainty of the strength of their sway over the course of events, willingness to sign the Association became "the litmus test for loyalty" to the Congress. Perhaps it was like a daily opinion poll that can be consoling — or disheartening — to a modern politican. The Congress provided machinery for distributing the Association for signing, as if they were determined to have the entire populace stand up and be counted. As a contemporary historian of the times described it, the Congress recommended that the General Committee "take effectual methods to have the Association signed throughout the province, and to demand from the non-subscribers the reasons for their refusal. Excepting in that part of the country included between the Broad and Saluda rivers, the non-subscribers were comparatively few," but these were to be "advertised as inimical to the liberties of America." If these few remained otherwise-minded, *their* liberty was not considered equally sacred: "Those who refused were disarmed, and few, who would not enter into any agreements for the publick security, were confined to their houses and plantations."[66]

The General Committee met on the issue of the stubborn "non-associators" and even ordered William Wragg, former chief justice who had never bent in his loyalty to the mother country, to take an oath not "to oppose the proceedings of the people." He refused, claiming the "right to exercise his own judgment...,although in doing so his sentiments might differ from the general voice." For that sin, the General Committee ordered him confined to his estate on the Ashley and later compelled him to leave the colony. En route to Amsterdam, his ship was driven ashore and he lost his life while trying to save an infant son. Thus perished a man who thought he, too, was committed to freedom — as did his persecutors.[67]

Other non-associators were persecuted too, although most were simply required to disarm themselves and remain in the limits of Charlestown. Their number there was small. A committee even had the temerity to call on William Bull at Ashley Hall for his signature. This hard-to-hate gentleman simply assured his visitors that "he wished as well to the country as any one" (which was true), and added — perhaps whimsically — that "even you gentlemen would look upon me in an odd light were I to subscribe an instrument of this kind."[68] And that ended that.

With the situation in the Charlestown area more or less in hand,[69] the Council of Safety — acting virtually as the ruling body of the province after the adjournment *sine die* of the Provincial Congress on June 22 — now turned to the remainder of the province: that large, thinly settled Back Country where the less genteel lived in an area as yet largely untouched by the America-England collision. Neither as wealthy nor as sophisticated as the only real town[70] of the province, the frontier area nevertheless contained the bulk of the white inhabitants. And they were hardly disciples of William Henry Drayton, Esq., Arthur Middleton, Esq., or the other gentlemen of the Council of Safety. Nor were frontiersmen in any rush to line up and sign the Association and thereby commit themselves to the cause led by planters who lived on their estates along the Ashley and the Cooper.

The chaos entered a whole new chapter involving considerable internal division and the threat of civil war as the Provincial Congress tried to make good its bid to be the spokesman for the citizens of South Carolina and for their liberty — constantly reiterating that what concerned them was liberty *within* the British Empire.

Footnotes, Chapter I

[1]For a short, clear narrative of this background, see Robert Weir, *"A Most Important Epocha": The Coming of the Revolution in South Carolina* (Columbia: University of South Carolina Press, 1970). The first chapter here seeks to compress this considerable background into a very few pages.

[2]The first extra-legal machinery to make protests against English policies goes back to December 4, 1773, when a meeting of citizens to resist the landing of tea gathered in the Great Hall over the Exchange. This led to a "General Meeting" on January 20, 1774, which began "systematizing and shaping the extra-legal organs of a new government." A new "General Committee" was to serve as a sort of steering committee between meetings. More attention recently has been devoted to the later General Meeting of July 6, 1774, which had delegates from all over the colony and which chose five delegates to the First Continental Congress which gathered in Philadelphia on September 5, 1774. This was "the parent of all government in South Carolina from that day to this...." It enlarged the General Committee to ninety-nine who served as a Committee of Correspondence and who summoned the First Provincial Congress and assigned to each district the number of representatives it should elect. As Professor D. D. Wallace put it, "Then was born the Legislature of what was soon to be the State of South Carolina, and a people so imbued with constitutional principles as to be able to call them into activity without one act of violence found themselves again under the direction of their elected representatives." For a summary of this evolution, see D. D. Wallace, *Life of Henry Laurens* (New York: Putnam, 1915), pp. 200-05.

[3]Jack P. Greene, "Bridge to Revolution: The Wilkes Fund Controversy in South Carolina, 1769-1775," in *Journal of Southern History*, XXIX (February, 1963), 29-52. For a shorter account of it, see Lewis P. Jones, *South Carolina: A Synoptic History for Laymen* (Columbia: Sandlapper Press, 1971), pp. 94 ff. Many members of the rebellious Provincial Congress were also members of the almost-defunct voice of the old Establishment, the Assembly.

[4]One of their dilemmas was that the events of 1688 were such an important part of the "constitution" that protected the "rights of Englishmen," and yet it was that same 1688 event, the Glorious Revolution, which had changed the constitution so as to bring about the supremacy of Parliament over king — that same parliament and its ministers whom they now were castigating in the 1760s and 1770s while professing continued loyalty to King, whose position had been so eroded ever since the constitutional revolution that had been won by the Whigs in 1688.

[5]Carl Bridenbaugh, *Myths and Realities: Societies of the Colonial South* (New York: Atheneum, 1963), chap. 3.

[6]David Duncan Wallace, *History of South Carolina* (3 vols.: New York: American Historical Society, 1934), II, 115-16; Edward McCrady, *History of South Carolina Under the Royal Government, 1719-1776* (New York: Macmillan Company, 1899; reprint: New York: Russell & Russell, 1969), p. 760, hereinafter cited as *S. C. Under Royal Gov't.* Wallace simply says it had the "great majority of the white population." Wallace, *History,* II, 117.

[7]The South Carolina gubernatorial candidate in 1974 who promised to return government "to the people" as it had been under "our forefathers two centuries ago" showed something less than an absolute mastery of history.

[8]McCrady, *S. C. Under Royal Gov't.,* p. 761.

[9]Wallace, *History,* II, 116. The list of members of the First Provincial Congress is in William Edwin Hemphill and Wylma Anne Wates (editors), *Extracts from the Journals of the Provincial Congresses of South Carolina, 1775-1776* (Columbia: South Carolina Archives Department, 1960), pp. 3-8; hereinafter cited as *Jour. Prov. Cong.,* a magnificent job of editing an invaluable source. Readers not acquainted with such useful but slightly read publications would be impressed and interested by the prefaces to this, pages vii-xxxiv.

[10]McCrady, *S.C. Under Royal Gov't.,* p. 794.

[11]*Ibid.,* p. 795.

[12]*Jour. Prov. Cong.* (January 17, 1775), pp. 28-29.

[13]*Ibid.,* p. 29. The Congress adjourned January 17 and did not meet again until June 1, 1775.

[14]*Ibid.,* p. 28. Delegates to the Continental Congress were Henry Middleton, Thomas Lynch, Christopher Gadsden, John Rutledge and Edward Rutledge.

[15]Writers about Drayton and this period constantly cite John Drayton, *Memoirs of the American Revolution, From Its Commencement to the Year 1776, Inclusive; as Relating to the State of South-Carolina, And Occasionally Refering to the States of North-Carolina and Georgia* (2 vols.: Charleston: A. E. Miller, 1821; reprinted: New York: Arno Press, 1969); hereinafter cited as Drayton, *Memoirs.* John Drayton was the son of William Henry Drayton and actually these are the memoirs of the father, based on papers, documents and manuscripts which the son inherited; see the son's explanation in the Preface. Although the *Memoirs* naturally present only one viewpoint and a rather prejudiced one at that, they cannot be

utilized alone; yet, they provide a tremendously valuable primary source. When William H. Drayton flashed like a meteor into the 1775 skies, he was only thirty-three years old; he was to die in 1779. For a biography, see William M. Dabney and Marion Dargan, *William Henry Drayton and the American Revolution* (Albuquerque: University of New Mexico Press, 1962).

[16]Weir, *Most Important Epocha*, p. 60.

[17]McCrady, *S. C. Under Royal Gov't*, p. 783.

[18]*Ibid.*, p. 784.

[19]McCrady (in *ibid.*, p. 751) holds that these speeches to grand juries had a tremendous influence in awakening many South Carolinians to the threat from the mother country.

[20]R. W. Gibbes (ed.), *Documentary History of the American Revolution: Consisting of Letters and Papers Relating to the Contest for Liberty, Chiefly in South Carolina, From Originals in the Possession of the Editor, And Other Sources* (3 vols.; New York: D. Appleton & Co., 1853-57; reprint: Spartanburg: Reprint Co., 1972), I, 71; hereinafter cited as Gibbes, *Doc. Hist.* Although Drayton and Dargan say (*Drayton*, p. 92) that Gibbes is "marred by errors," the reader will find it cited here quite frequently, partially because it is most convenient and also because the writer has not found the errors. Certainly much of it is the same as Drayton's *Memoirs*, which was one of the major sources used by Gibbes.

[21]Drayton, *Memoirs*, I, 221. Adopted January 16, 1775.

[22]Drayton, *ibid.*, has the above words italicized. This provided "legal" justification for such later action as intercepting or seizing mail and other communications. The text of this is not included in the *Extracts from the Journals of the Provincial Congresses.*

[23]The State House stood where now stands the Charleston Courthouse.

[24]Drayton, *Memoirs*, I, 223.

[25]Both pieces of correspondence in Drayton, *Memoirs*, I, 224-25.

[26]Wallace, *Henry Laurens*, p. 205.

[27]Drayton, *Memoirs*, I, 226-28. The contraption must have looked like a modern float and apparently (if one believes Drayton) must have brought more glee to the spectators than do the floats of a Santa Claus parade now.

[28]Quoted from British Public Records by Wallace, *History*, II, 121.

[29]Many yet fail to realize that war began fourteen months before the Declaration of Independence. Many historians now speak of "the Revolution" as beginning about 1763, and talk of a different episode, "the Revolutionary War," a 1775-1783 affair.

[30]On adjournment in January, it left such decision to "the Charles-Town General Committee." *Jour. Prov. Cong.*, p. 30. Previously it had been scheduled to meet June 20. McCrady, *S. C. Under Royal Gov't.*, pp. 789-90.

[31]Col. Charles Pinckney (1731-82) had been a respected judge and was reluctant to participate in the Revolution. After the fall of Charlestown in 1780, he took British protection — for which he was later penalized by loss of twelve percent of his estate. He was father of Charles Pinckney, who served four terms as governor of the state and was a member of the Federal Constitutional Convention. He was a cousin of Charles Cotesworth Pinckney.

[32]Cited in Wallace, *History*, II, 122.

[33]Eric F. Goldman, "Firebrands of the Revolution," in *National Geographic*, CXLVI (July, 1974), 12. He gives a stirring summary of the great change and the agreed objective of differing Americans — what they shared and which he calls "The Idea." Se especially *ibid.*, pp. 12-13.

[34]*Jour. Prov. Cong.* (June 2, 1775), p. 34.

[35]By a vote of 23 to 25, members of the General Committee refused to commit themselves in May. McCrady, *S. C. Under Royal Gov't.*, p. 791.

[36]Text in *Jour. Prov. Cong.*, p. 36; also, in Drayton, *Memoirs*, I, 285-86. Copy of this on page 41.

[37]For text of Laurens' eloquent appeal, see Wallace, *Laurens*, pp. 207 *ff.* A short extract carrying its mood is in Wallace, *History*, II, 122. It is interesting that Drayton, the most radical member of the body, perhaps, does not mention Laurens' speech in his account; see Drayton, *Memoirs*, I, 254-55.

[38]*Jour. Prov. Cong.* (June 22, 1775), p. 66.

[39]McCrady, *S. C. Under Royal Gov't.*, p. 793. Also, see text in "Papers of the General Committee, Etc.," in *S. C. Historical Magazine*, VIII (July, 1907), 141-42.

[40]*Jour. Prov. Cong.*, pp. 50, 51, 52. The members chosen reflected the varying impetuosity of members of Congress: Henry Laurens, the moderate, was president; the moderates or cautious members included Benjamin Elliott, Rawlins Lowndes, and Charles Pinckney. More radical were the two friends and neighbors, William Henry Drayton and Arthur Middleton.

[41]On claiming control over the militia, see *ibid.*, pp. 44, 54, 55-56.

[42]*Ibid.*, p. 33.

[43]For biographical information, see *Dictionary of American Biography*, III, 464-65; Wallace, *History*, II, 122-23. The poor man, staying temporarily in the home of Miles Brewton on King Street, found himself oppressed and puzzled by the headaches which he had inherited, discussing them with a sympathetic Brewton. See Drayton, *Memoirs*, I, 262-63. Campbell had married Sarah, daughter of Ralph Izard in 1763.

[44]Text in *Jour. Prov. Cong.*, pp. 59-60; Drayton, *Memoirs*, I, 259-61; also, in Appendix. It was labeled a "humble Address and Declaration of the Provincial Congress," and was delivered in person by designated members.

[45]*Jour. Prov. Cong.*, p. 60. For text of "Declaration of the Causes and Necessity of Taking up Arms," see Henry Steele Commager (ed.), *Documents of American History* (8th ed.; 2 vols.; New York: Appleton-Century-Crofts, 1968), I, 92-95.

[46]*Jour. Prov. Cong.*, p. 65.

[47]His home still stands on Tradd Street.

[48]Apparently Stuart was not the monster that his enemies professed they believed him to be, and the whole affair is a historiographical controversy too big for this space. See Philip M. Hamer, "John Stuart's Indian Policy During the Early Months of the American Revolution," in *Miss. Valley Historical Review*, XVII (December, 1930), 351-66; also, Communication of D. D. Wallace in *S. C. Hist. Magazine*, XLVII (July, 1946), 190-92.

[49]*Jour. Prov. Cong.*, p. 64.

[50]Drayton, *Memoirs*, I, 293; full text, pp. 292-96.

[51]Wallace, *History*, II, 125-27. For more on Stuart's attitude, see Joseph Habersham to Philotheon Chiffelle, June 16, 1775, in Gibbes, *Doc. Hist.*, I, 102-04. Stuart had suggested to Cameron that he "use[his] influence to dispose those people to act in defence of his Majesty and Government, if found necessary." Although such could have an innocuous meaning, Drayton put the worst implications on this Stuart letter written in January. This led the Secret Committee to demand that Stuart send to them all of his official correspondence, which he did not do — and said he could not.

[52]William Legge, second Earl of Dartmouth, British colonial secretary.

[53]Dabney and Dargan, *Drayton,* p. 76. Alexander Innes, loyal secretary to Campbell, said that "this Province hardly falls short of Massachusetts in every indecency, violence and contempt to Government," *Ibid.* For another account of the summer excitement over Stuart, see Dabney and Dargan, *Drayton,* pp. 79-81.

[54]Dabney and Dargan, *Drayton,* pp. 40-44. This account seems to indicate that Stuart was defending both the law and the Indians and that he was upheld by the Council which canceled Drayton's lease of Catawba lands.

[55]Stuart to William Bull, February 11, 1775, in Drayton, *Memoirs,* I, 235-36.

[56]Quoted in Dabney and Dargan, *Drayton,* p. 80.

[57]*Ibid.,* p. 84. The letters purloined from the post offices — and the substitutes then sent along in their place — are printed in Drayton, *Memoirs,* I, 346-50.

[58]*Jour. Prov. Cong.* (February 3, 1776), pp. 173-74.

[59]The message to the Catawbas in Journal of the Council of Safety, in S. C. Historical Society *Collections,* II (1858), 32-34; this very significant document is hereinafter cited as SCHS *Collections.*

[60]Dabney and Dargan, *Drayton,* p. 75.

[61]*Ibid.,* p. 75. Also, see Gary D. Olson, "Loyalists and the American Revolution: Thomas Brown and the South Carolina Backcountry, 1775-1776," in *South Carolina Historical Magazine,* LXVIII (October, 1967), p. 203; hereinafter cited as "Loyalists and the Amer. Rev." The letter from Lee had arrived May 3. D. D. Wallace is not very charitable to Lee; see his Communication, *S. C. Hist. Magazine,* XLVII, 190-92.

[62]Bridenbaugh, *Myths and Realities,* p. 64, based on William A. Schaper, *Sectionalism and Representation in South Carolina,* p. 309.

[63]Jour. of Cou. of Safety (July 13, 1775), SCHS *Collections,* II, 37.

[64]Jour. of Cou. of Safety (July 15, 1775), in SCHS *Collections,* II, 43. Burnett allegedly had been holding meetings "under the sanction of religion." See Thomas Hutchinson to Council of Safety, July 5, 1775, in *ibid.,* II, 70-71.

[65]Wallace, *History,* II, 128. Laurens had even protested the whipping of a slave where there was no clear proof of guilt. See Wallace, *Laurens,* p. 214.

[66]David Ramsay, *History of the Revolution of South Carolina, From a British Province to an Independent State* (2 vols.; Trenton: Isaac Collins, 1785), I, 42.

[67]Edward McCrady, *History of South Carolina in the Revolution, 1775-1780* (New York: Macmillan Co., 1901; reprint: New York: Russell & Russell, 1969), pp. 27-29; hereinafter cited as *S. C., Revol., 1775-80* (since a subsequent volume with the same title covered 1780-83). Writing at the end of the nineteenth century, McCrady reflects considerable indignation and intolerance of Drayton and his group; see *ibid.,* pp. 23-32.

[68]*Ibid.,* pp. 29-30.

[69]Ramsay said that in Charleston only forty refused to sign. *Hist. of Revol. in S. C.,* I, 42.

[70]This assumes that one neglects the other "towns" usually noted — but still only villages — such as Camden, Georgetown and Beaufort.

Chapter Two
Conservative Frontiersmen

Thus far, this narrative has been concerned with the *political* story of a people meandering down a road leading to revolution. Such is always dangerous business at best within any body politic, but it is doubly dangerous to treat a people as a body politic when actually it is not. And such was the case if one speaks of South Carolina in 1775, for actually there was not one South Carolina — but two.

In theory, perhaps, there was only one South Carolina if one refers to the colonial political organization or to the clique of practicing politicos in Charlestown. But South Carolina was composed of two distinct societies without a close intermixing of the two. Such has always been the case, but there was perhaps a more marked and dangerous schism on the eve of the Revolution than at any other point in colonial or state history.

The events heretofore depicted were acted out primarily within the coastal area and society often referred to as "fabled" by some who speak more accurately than they realize. For the first half century after the founding of Charlestown (1670), that region "was walled in on the south and west by redskins and Latins," and its "unusually slow-growing population rendered any extension of its boundaries needless."[1] Homogeneous in flavor and occupation, its spread by 1750 had still been mostly along the coast and had come to include the plantation areas around Georgetown and Beaufort.[2] Hub of this city-state was the only American metropolis south of Philadelphia, one that had about 12,000 people by 1775. All roads seemed to radiate from Charlestown,[3] a town that had "developed nearly every business facility needed to serve a rich agricultural hinterland" — not just with necessities, but even "'European Goods fit for the Season' to delight plantation womenfolk."[4]

Prior to 1775, there had been marked prosperity: Between 1740 and 1776, rice exports grew threefold and indigo fourfold; between 1734 and 1774, the value of Carolina produce jumped from £100,000 to over £500,000 while large plantations with slave labor became firmly rooted. By 1750, bustling Charlestown had become the center of the entire economic, cultural and political life of the "Carolina Society," a term not properly applied yet to the region along the Fall Line or westward of it. At that time, in this Low Country of about 11,000 square miles, approximately 110,000 people lived. Of these, 97,000 were rural — and of these, only twenty-six percent were white. Despite one urban center, the density of population was only nine per square mile.[5]

The Low Country was a "land of opportunity" for a few entrepreneurs and the large planters,[6] and "in per capita wealth and income, Low Country whites led all Americans."[7]

The Golden Age was not to come to coastal Carolina until after Independence, but the new wealth was nevertheless evident in splendor and style. This is not the place to elaborate on theaters, concerts, horse racing, town houses or other manifestations of culture. In recent years, some scholars have been so sacrilegious as to suggest that perhaps before 1776 there was still more dilettantism than genuine culture, more lip service to education than to real learning, more materialism than humanism. But hardly any frontier society can be expected to develop a cultural utopia within fifty to seventy years of its founding on the rim of a new, unexplored wilderness. Schools of an elementary sort were available — to those who could and would pay for them. Sometimes the bigwigs procured some learning for themselves but neglected it for the rest of their society. Despite the later improvements, before 1775 "reading was never a favorite recreation, nor was learning highly prized for its own sake."[8] Alcoholism was a genuine problem, and partying was more popular than philosophizing about the Age of Reason. David Ramsay, a resident of the town, revealed some of the warts of his neighborhood as well as its beauty spots, and a New England visitor cut sharply to the point: "Cards, dice, the bottle and horses engross prodigious portions of time and attention: the gentlemen (planters and merchants) are mostly men of the turf and gamesters."[9] Dr. Alexander Garden was no more complimentary about "the gentleman planters, who are absolutely above every occupation but eating, drinking, lolling, smoking, and sleeping, which five modes constitute the essence of their life and existence."[10] Fortunately, such traits were not universal.

This aristocratic society of the Low Country with "plenty of the Good Things of Life" numbered about two thousand dominant whites. The gentry were intelligent and were usually "men of mild temper" who were drawn to agriculture "because it seemed to offer the most lucrative rewards and guaranteed the greatest social approval." Success in agriculture was the road to wealth — and one that did not require a great knowledge of farming but only the original capital and slave labor. Their society and environment shaped them — and shaped them to be leaders.

Perhaps it is best to describe this interesting and able group as an aristocracy still in the making. Just as in England the ruling gentry of the seventeenth century had dominated the various facets of society and all major institutions, including politics, so did the corresponding class in Carolina expect to play such a leadership role here. Being small in number and totally dominant in the sparsely settled city-state of the Low Country, by 1750 they were in full control — not only of society, but also of the Commons House of Assembly and the Council. But after 1750, a veritable flood of new settlers poured into the Back Country — coming not via Charlestown nor on the crest of a westward-moving frontier, but seeping steadily southward from inland Pennsylvania and frontier Virginia. The coastal gentry welcomed the flood: They were potential customers and a bulwark against the Indians. Even so, there were no particularly close relations yet between the two, the "Pine Barrens" serving as a buffer zone between the aristocracy of the coast and rude frontiersmen along the fall line and in the Piedmont. With their own opulence the Establishment was too preoccupied, and the Assembly failed to provide any local government. After all, it was a city-state. "No matter where a man lived, he had to go to Charleston for justice." Nor did the burgeoning population of "the west" acquire any seats at all in a parliament still designed for a city-state — for "the town" and its "suburbs," the nearby Anglican parishes.[11]

By any yardstick of comparison, the newer Carolinians differed from those on the coast — those who made something of a fetish of being gentlemen carved from the English pattern to which they self-consciously clung.[12] The Back Country contained Germans (often called "Dutch"), who settled around Orangeburg, Saxe-Gotha (modern Lexington) and the Dutch Fork (between the Broad and

Saluda rivers). Even more numerous were the Scotch-Irish, along the streams of the Piedmont. Near the coast, the Anglican Church was strong with the plutocracy; in the Back Country, it was the Presbyterian and the Baptist. Here were not planters but subsistence farmers — with an occasional big and successful farmer showing signs of becoming an entrepreneur. Moses Kirkland, for example, owned thousands of acres in thirty-six tracts, but in contrast with big landholders in the tidewater area, he had only thirty-six slaves.[13] The phobia about black slave rebellions did not grip the Piedmont with a constant fear, but concern about the red men was another matter. Catawbas inhabited present York County along the Catawba River, and the more powerful and numerous Cherokees lived west of the "Indian line" (approximately the present western border of Spartanburg, Laurens and Abbeville counties).[14]

Insofar as there were Back Country settlements, they bore the names of streams in their neighborhoods, as did many of the churches and meeting houses. Speeding motorists today flash by signs of meandering waters which mean little to them but which once designated also little clusters of eighteenth-century neighbors: Lawson's Fork (a creek as well as a neighborhood), King's Creek, Indian Creek, the Congarees, and others. But as for towns and specific communities or even bustling villages in the Back Country, there were none.

Differing peoples can live within the same jurisdiction with equanimity, but in the eighteenth century there was serious friction between the two South Carolinas, upper and lower, not because one was wealthier than the other, but because one enjoyed the privileges, advantages and — above all — political control. The older faction, a minority, ruled the majority. The cards appeared stacked. A snobbishness or unconcern was but thinly veiled, as were the resentment and irritation.

In the 1770s, the quarrels between England and her colony simply sharpened the problems and friction which had already erupted clamorously within South Carolina during the 1760s. The Back Country, devoid of organization, had then generated the "Regulator" movement[15] to cope with problems that had come simply because "the gentlemen" of the colonial government had not deigned to extend government into their lawless wilderness. Not only did the Scotch-Irish lack even a semblance of local government, but also — as has been noted — they lacked any voice, representation or influence in the government of the colony. To make matters worse, the vacuum created by lack of government, as Historian Carl Bridenbaugh aptly put it, "immediately sucked in most of the lawless and disorderly characters of the entire South,"[16] and thus in the absence of law enforcement, judiciary and jails, the Regulators necessarily took "the law" into their own hands to protect bona fide settlers from rogues and villains.[17] By 1767, civil war threatened when the frustrated, Regulator-minded Back Country reached the verge of descending on Charlestown in force. At first the Anglican curmudgeon, the Reverend Charles Woodmason, besought the seething frontiersmen to settle for a Remonstrance, but he, too, quickly lost patience, "Finding that they were only amus'd and trifled with, all Confidence of the Poor in the Great is destroy'd and I believe will never exist again." Disgusted with the "humane gentlemen" of the Carolina Society, he attacked them in a letter to Henry Laurens: "Have Patience, have Patience has for many Years been the preoccupation of our Political Quacks, to the Country People. Their Patients have applied the Anondyne, till they are become Paralytic and require more sovereign Remedies."[18]

In mild response, the Assembly gave an aspirin to the Back Country for its alarmingly high fever: creation of six new judicial districts with a circuit court in each. The large inland districts were Cheraws, Camden, Orangeburg and Ninety Six. It was too little and too late. As Woodmason lamented, they still had to go several hundred miles to the city to sue for £3 or to take out a marriage license, and he still lived "in Dred of Villains robbing my House, steal'g my Horses and Cattel, ravishing my Wife and Daughrs." A recent historian of a county in Ninety Six District noted, "Those who wished to resort to the law still had to file their pleadings with the clerk in Charleston. All writs were issued from Charleston, and all estates were administered there."[19] And there was no Interstate 26 by which the litigant from Newberry could whiz down to Charleston.

Creation of courthouses at places like Camden and Ninety Six (distant themselves from many of their constituents) did not touch the problem of representation in the Assembly which continued to be based on the parish system. Most of the Back Country was in the huge St. Mark or St. Frederick parishes, which meant that the polling places were virtually inaccessible to citizens burdened by an inequitable system that manifested clearly a scandalous example of "taxation without representation." Gadsden, Drayton and others knew that phrase well as they roared it against English ministries, but they failed to appreciate the view from Ninety Six.

When the Back Country heard from the "Sons of Liberty" gathered at the "Liberty Tree" at Charlestown, they were probably cynical. If they felt oppression, and they thought they did, they knew where the oppressors were — and it was not London. Nor did they care about the contest of the Commons House versus the Council and governor: They resented the Assembly more than they did the English, whose deeds and philosophy affected them not at all. Better to cope with the sins of which they knew than to tilt with even more distant windmills.

Perhaps the political inequity would have been easier to accept if there had been more amenities of life in the Back Country, but life was hard. Roads were few — and bad. For a large-but-scattered population, churches (or "meeting houses") were scarce and inadequate. Schools were practically non-existent among the rude and unlettered populace. Woodmason observed that

> just to humour a few Noisy Bell weathers and swaggerers, who bellow for Liberty, the Assembly has in recent years spent not less than £20,000 on the ballroom it calls the Exchange, a statue of William Pitt, the Wilkes fund, and the trips of Christopher Gadsden..., while it denies schools and churches, roads and bridges to the upcountry![20]

Although the Back Country majority did not then subscribe to the revolutionary protests of the Provincial Congress, they were not the only Carolinians wavering. There were various others who were cool on the new radicalism for various reasons. The whole business of just who the Loyalists were — as if they were by definition the non-conformists of the 1770s — has attracted many scholars recently. Robert W. Barnwell, Jr., has been the principal South Carolina scholar on this topic and has noted several classes and several explanations for Loyalists in general: (1) Obvious would be the "official class" and the placemen, beholden to the Ministry and ethically obligated; (2) the Anglican clergy, although in South Carolina they more often sympathized with their parishioners than with Whitehall;[21] (3) the Scots, often a wealthy group, often merchants affiliated with establishments in the United Kingdom, and often recent arrivals (since 1763) and hence still Scots and not yet South Carolinians;[22] (4) a merchant class, often factors with trade ties that would be seriously strained by political turmoil. Even in the Low Country there was a shrinking body of moderates hard to classify. At first they were repelled by American radicals, "But each coercive step of the British had the effect of forcing the moderates into the ranks of the radicals."[23]

But it was the Back Countrymen along their creeks and around a few crossroad stores who were really crucial as events moved to an awesome showdown. Maybe the coastal plutocracy had nobody to blame but themselves: If the Back Country had been properly represented in the Assembly for the ten years prior to 1775 during the wrangles with England, if they had been present at the harangues under the Liberty Tree, or if they had participated in the debates in Broad Street taverns, then the Back Countrymen "would probably have had the same attitudes as the planters on the coast."[24] Instead, they were "tuned in to a different channel" — or not tuned in at all. As Barnwell put it so well, their minds just had not been prepared for the Revolution, and their absences from the Assembly or other dialogues in Charlestown explain that. Hence, "the general distrust of low country leaders took the form of 'let the low country fight its own battles' rather than one of active Loyalism."[25] In their own way, they, too, were prospering and "not inclined to involve themselves in a revolution upon abstract principles of government, in which they were not interested."[26]

It was this discontented Back Country horde to whom the Provincial Congress now was to turn for support and backing in the summer of 1775. The response they received from that inland quarter was not encouraging.

The Charlestown revolutionary party by July 1775 knew that absolutely crucial to their success in luring the frontier over to their cause was the militia. There were two reasons for the great importance of this group: First, obviously the loyalty or attitude of any military group was essential to any self-proclaimed government; second, in the absence of genuine local government in the Back Country, the militia represented the symbol of authority and it was to militia officers and magistrates that the people naturally looked for leadership, there being no political leaders in their neighborhood.

The Council of Safety therefore occupied itself much with things military. First, it created three new militia regiments itself — the "provincial" troops. There were two infantry regiments, commanded by colonels Christopher Gadsden and William Moultrie; there was also the Ranger regiment (cavalry), led by Colonel William Thomson.[27] The colonels were authorized to organize additional volunteer companies and permit election of officers by these volunteers.[28]

WILLIAM MOULTRIE

CHRISTOPHER GADSDEN

Two of the new infantry regiments created by the Council of Safety were commanded by colonels William Moultrie and Christopher Gadsden. Gadsden's fame, however, rests principally on his Charleston agitation against British policy prior to 1776.

The existing, or "regular," militia had been established earlier under royal government auspices and it was now essential to the Council to determine its attitude toward the course being pursued by the Continental Congress. Consisting of ten to fourteen thousand men, it was loosely organized along regional lines into twelve infantry regiments and one cavalry. In 1775 it was not overwhelmingly committed to either side in the Revolution then beginning, the individuals within it being themselves divided. Insofar as possible, the Congress hoped to "bring it over" (nobody used the word "defecting"), and many militiamen without changing their organization did come to serve the revolutionary leaders.[29] Some whole units made that transfer; for example, most of the regiment commanded by Colonel Richard Richardson became a mainstay in the support of the Provincial Congress.

Events of the summer gave ample proof that the Council of Safety was prudent to worry about militia colonels who might not be lending support to the radical cause. Area of greatest concern was the fork between the Broad and Saluda rivers. Here the Upper Saluda Regiment was under the command of Colonel Thomas Fletchall, who lived on Fairforest Creek in what is now Union County.[30] Because of rumors of his own lack of enthusiasm for the revolutionary party, his conduct "gave great uneasiness" to the Council of Safety, and hence it was decided to try to get him to join up forthrightly or at least make plainly known his sentiments. A colonel of the militia was too important to ignore: He might well carry his whole area into the Loyalist camp and into active opposition.

Accordingly, the Council on July 15, 1775, approved a lengthy letter to Colonel Fletchall, a diplomatic but pointed document designed to lure him into taking a position since "we are anxiously desirous of enrolling the number of our friends upon whom we may firmly rely for aid in the day of trial."[31] As Henry Laurens phrased this epistle, "I must intimate, that common fame has transmitted intelligence...that Col. Fletchall, a gentleman of considerable influence..., is not a friend to the cause of liberty." Reassuring the colonel that such charges against a distinguished and wise man — here so flattered — were patently unlikely, they asked

> an open and explicit declaration, of the part you now take, and mean to take...; whether you choose to join the friends of the glorious cause of freedom...or to aid and abet the tools of despotism, the only dangerous enemies of our misguided Sovereign Lord, the King?

Reprinted from *Ninety Six* by Carl Julien and H. L. Watson, page 67, by permission of the University of South Carolina Press. Copyright 1950 by the University of South Carolina Press.

Yarborough's Mill was situated on the Laurens County side of the Enoree River. Across the river on the Spartanburg County side, where Cedar Shoals Creek enters the river, was J. W. Ford's place. Here a major confrontation took place in which most of Colonel Fletchall's Loyalist followers refused to commit themselves to the Revolutionary "Association."

To smoke Fletchall out, the Council sent him a copy of the Association to sign. If he were to do that, they asked that he further seek to get as many other signers as he could and to send them in monthly. (It may have appeared to him like being asked to be the colonel to head up the United Fund which he had reportedly been criticizing.)

The Council concluded by reporting a rumor that Fletchall reputedly was being tempted by "the malevolent artifices of ministerial hirelings in this metropolis" and by the risk of losing his positions as colonel and magistrate. Although the straight-faced Council could "hardly entertain an opinion that such paltry considerations could have had weight with a gentleman of your understanding," they did note (or warn) that the time was near at hand when such would not be "productive either of honor or profit to the holder." As evidence, they reported losses of nine hundred killed among "ministerial forces" to one hundred Americans killed on June 17. (This referred to Bunker Hill.)

At the very time the Council was dispatching this letter to Fletchall, he had his troops gathered at their mustering ground at John Ford's farm on the Enoree River. (The site was at the point where Cedar Shoals Creek enters the Enoree at the present Spartanburg-Union line, the location of the later Battle of Musgrove's Mill in August 1780.) There were 1,500 men present, according to Drayton, including some from nearby regiments.[32] This proved to be a crucial meeting: Drayton judged that it promoted the whole area's disaffection toward the Revolutionary cause, although it may be going too far to say — as Drayton charged — "the real purpose...was to organize the men against the revolution."[33] Fletchall read the Association to the troops — but in such a way, it was said, as to reveal his disapproval of it. Not a single man signed it.

At this point, a "Counter-Association" was brought forward by Loyalist-leaning Joseph Robinson and most of the people signed it.[34] This was in effect a declaration of neutrality which continued an allegiance to the King but also expressed a desire "to live in peace and true friendship with the rest of our countrymen notwithstanding our aforesaid diversity of opinions." The only laws they agreed to respect were those of Britain and the Assembly. Such strategy reputedly came from Governor Campbell, and even Drayton conceded that if His Majesty's Governor had promptly gone himself to the interior, "the whole proceedings of the Provincial Congress would have been overthrown."[35] (Drayton's laconic explanation for the Governor's immobility: "Providence had not so directed his actions....") If he had so bestirred himself and ventured forth, Campbell might also have strengthened the hand of conservative members of the radical faction like Rawlins Lowndes.[36]

Returning home, Fletchall found the letter from the Council of Safety and had the difficult task of responding on July 24. In his reply, he reported about the muster and the failure of the Association to attract any subscribers, and also told of Robinson's "Counter-Association." He expressed regret that the Council apparently viewed him "as an enemy to my country" but stated that he was "resolved, and do utterly refuse to take up arms against my king."[37]

This reply from the major personage between the Broad and Saluda must have alarmed the Council of Safety, but even more drastic action than letters going back and forth was taking place. Also, something transpired at the muster at Ford's which Fletchall did not chronicle. About three weeks earlier, the Council had directed Major James Mayson, second in command of the Provincial Rangers regiment, to take possession of Fort Charlotte on the Savannah River (above Augusta). With captains John Caldwell and Moses Kirkland, the mission was accomplished, and by July 14 Mayson and Kirkland had moved the military stores captured to the Ninety Six Courthouse where there was practically no protection for them.[38]

At this point, Captain Moses Kirkland defected, thus beginning a rather romantic career as well as strenuous efforts to promote greater militancy among the Back Country people, hitherto either passive or neutralist.

Like so many decisions that involved picking sides in the 1770s, Kirkland's switch did not stem from deep political philosophy, wide reading and study or intense commitment. Just as Drayton had resented placemen, now Kirkland resented his superior officers and felt that his captaincy in the Provincial Militia was not proper recognition of his worth and importance. Further, he had an old grudge against Major Mayson, his superior, for both rank and Back Country influence. Knowing that Colonel Fletchall was holding the general muster at Ford's on the Enoree, he sent a message to him (by one Terry) saying that if the colonel would send men to seize the stores at Ninety Six he (Kirkland) would not oppose the raid. With timidity typical of him, Fletchall hesitated, but was persuaded by the strong personalities around him to take advantage of the opportunity. Two hundred men were dispatched from the conclave on the Enoree (Fletchall did not himself go) to Ninety Six where, as promised, on July 17 they encountered no opposition and absconded with the supplies and ammunition. Thus the stores and munitions changed hands for the third time in days — from royal to revolutionary to neutralist owners. The neutralist — or King's cause — was also further strengthened, for Kirkland also came over to Fletchall's forces.[39]

This new recruit for the King's Men had come to South Carolina from the North in 1752, settling first on the west side of the Catawba. There were rumors that he was not too outstanding — accusations of selling rum to Indians and harboring runaway slaves. Ultimately he acquired many tracts of land in Orangeburg and Ninety Six districts, his best plantation and home being on Turkey Creek in present Edgefield County. He had been a leading participant in the Regulator movement and also a magistrate.[40]

Another recruit who now also brought strong anti-radical feelings to the Fletchall faction was Thomas Brown, one of the most intriguing personalities of the period. Having arrived in America early in 1774[41] on a chartered trip with seventy-four indentured servants, he soon was conducting successful and large farming operations along the Broad River in northeastern Georgia upriver from Augusta. Young and rash, he had the bad judgment to heckle a radical meeting, an affront for which he was unmercifully treated under the pressure of intolerance which so often grips emotion-laden controversy. There is a dispute as to his fate: Either he was tarred and feathered, or his feet were severely burned. Whatever the brutal persecution, it made a flaming Loyalist out of him.[42] Now joining the Fletchall entourage, like Kirkland he added backbone to the Back Country faction who had an indecisive leader as their colonel.

Such recruits for Fletchall's followers did not augur well for the gentlemen of the Provincial Congress in Charlestown. The Back Country was picking sides, and South Carolinians were not uniting in a massive anti-England, anti-ministerial movement. Along the creeks obviously lived many King's Men — perhaps passive, but nonetheless not friends of radicalism or of precipitant secession.

Footnotes, Chapter II

[1]Bridenbaugh, *Myths and Realities,* p. 55. Chapter II, "Carolina Society," of that book is the basis of the brief characterization which follows here. For suggestions of social and institutional history of the eighteenth century which is available, see Lewis P. Jones, *Books and Articles on South Carolina History: A List for Laymen* (Columbia: University of South Carolina Press, 1970), chap. 7.

[2]A few pushed inland to the townships around modern Kingstree, St. Matthews and Orangeburg, but they were hardly made from the Charlestown mold.

[3]As a glance at the now-often-reproduced maps of Henry Mouzon and James Cook shows.

[4]Bridenbaugh, *Myths and Realities,* p. 59.

[5]*Ibid.,* p. 61.

[6]Henry Middleton, for example, had an estate of 50,000 acres and 800 slaves. Henry Laurens, son of a saddler, himself a merchant and then also a planter, came to have 20,000 acres. Even John Stuart, the Indian agent, acquired over 15,000 acres and 200 slaves. Bridenbaugh, *Myths and Realities,* p. 67. John Drayton, father of William Henry Drayton, had 13,718½ acres. M. Eugene Sirmans, "South Carolina Royal Council, 1720-1763," in *William and Mary Quarterly,* XVIII (July, 1961), 392.

[7]Bridenbaugh, *Myths and Realities,* p. 67.

[8]*Ibid.,* p. 103.

[9]Josiah Quincy, Jr., quoted in *ibid.,* p. 84.

[10]Quoted in *ibid.,* p. 113.

[11]1790 Census: Population of Low Country (the three judicial districts along the coast, the old "Carolina Society" area): Whites, 28,644; Blacks, 79,216; the Up Country: Whites, 111,534; Blacks, 29,679. William A. Schaper, "Sectionalism and Representation in South Carolina," in American Historical Association *Annual Report,* 1901, Vol. I (reprint: New York: Da Capo Press, 1968), Plate II, opposite page 378. At home, the English did not adjust Parliamentary representation to changing population patterns, as students who recall "the Great Reform Bill of 1832" are aware.

[12]Again, for an incisive and highly readable view of the area, read Carl Bridenbaugh, "The Back Settlements," chap. 3 in *Myths and Realities.* For other suggestions, see Jones, *Books and Articles,* chap. 7.

[13]Robert W. Barnwell, "Loyalism in South Carolina, 1765-1785." unpublished Ph.D. dissertation, Duke University, 1941, p. 8. Another general study which has much less on South Carolina than does Barnwell is Robert M. Calhoon, *Loyalists in Revolutionary America, 1760-1781* (Harcourt Brace Jovanovich, 1965). The chapter 41, "Low Country Unity and Back Country Civil War in South Carolina, 1775-1776," leans heavily on the article by Gary D. Olson, already cited.

[14]The Cherokee area extended across the North Carolina mountains and into modern Tennessee.

[15]Not to be confused with the North Carolina Regulators, formed to oppose a government unpopular with many North Carolinians. South Carolina Regulators were formed because of the absence of government.

[16]Bridenbaugh, *Myths and Realities,* p. 163.

[17]For a vivid description of conditions, see excerpts from the Journal of the Reverend Charles Woodmason, quoted in Bridenbaugh, *Myths and Realities,* pp. 164-65. The Journal is now available in a recent edition: Charles Woodmason, *Carolina Backcountry on the Eve of the Revolution,* ed. Richard J. Hooker (Chapel Hill: University of North Carolina Press, 1953).

[18]Quoted by Bridenbaugh, *Myths and Realities,* p. 166.

[19]Thomas H. Pope, *History of Newberry County South Carolina* (2 vols.; Columbia: University of South Carolina Press, 1973), I, 44.

[20]Bridenbaugh, *Myths and Realities,* p. 167.

[21]There were twenty Anglican ministers in South Carolina in 1775 — mostly in the inflamed Low Country. Only five returned to England or refused to take the oath. Barnwell, "Loyalism in S. C.," p. 30.

[22]Prominent were Alexander Garden, Robert Wells and Alexander Hewatt. The latter was a Presbyterian minister who returned home and then wrote a useful history of South Carolina with an admittedly Loyalist point of view.

[23]Barnwell, "Loyalism in S. C.," p. 35. This scholar coped with the reason that South Carolina conservatives and moderates could not prevent the colony from following other colonies. There seemed little reason for South Carolina to secede: they were enjoying prosperity; their military weakness was obvious; they were badly divided; they could not prove real injury from imperial policy; ministerial stupidity was more of a threat to the future rather than being real and present danger.

Certainly all these factors dictated loyalism, not secession. Why then should such a conservative crew turn into revolutionaries? Simply because there was no middle course available: it was a matter of join the shrill others, or accept submission — and whatever they were, they were not eager to be known as "submissionists" to anybody. Barnwell, "Loyalism," pp. 46-47. Also for an interpretation, see Calhoon, *Loyalists in Revol. Amer.*, pp. 448-52.

[24]Barnwell, "Loyalism in S. C.," p. 140. McCrady also has some interesting "what if?" suppositions about alternative English actions which might have avoided the collision; see *S.C. Under Royal Gov't.*, pp. 795-96. One might oversimplify by saying that the Revolution was caused by inept British statesmanship and unwise statesmen. Calhoon stresses that Campbell encouraged Fletchall and the Back Country to resist but to avoid a direct conflict or collision until British regular troops could be brought to the area to counter the Whigs. Calhoon, *Loyalists in Revol. Amer.*, p. 456.

[25]Barnwell, "Loyalism in S. C.," p. 142.

[26]McCrady, *S. C. Under Royal Gov't.*, p. 797.

[27]The combined strength of the infantry forces on July 15 was 470. See report of William Moultrie in Journal of Council of Safety, in SCHS *Collections*, II, 47-48. The Journals of the Council and of the Provincial Congress both show that these bodies spent much of their time on things military, including such matters even as uniforms, insignia, flags and the manual of arms.

[28]Jour. of Cou. of Safety (July 21, 1775), in SCHS *Collections*, II, 54.

[29]Wallace, *History,* II, 124-25. For the organization of regular militia, the districts and a list of officers, see McCrady, *S. C. in Revol., 1775-80,* pp. 11-12. On the new Provincial militia, *ibid.,* pp. 12-16.

[30]His area of command embraced the present counties of Spartanburg, Union and Laurens. See J. B. O. Landrum, *Colonial and Revolutionary History of Upper South Carolina* (Greenville: Shannon & Co., 1897; reprint: Spartanburg: Reprint Co., 1959), p. 46; hereinafter cited as *Col. and Revol. Hist.*

[31]Letter in Jour. of Cou. of Safety, in SCHS *Collections*, II, 40-43.

[32]Drayton, *Memoirs,* I, 323; Barnwell, "Loyalism in S. C.," p. 101. Barnwell says the whole region from the Broad to the Savannah was represented. The regimental muster took place July 13-16, 1775.

[33]Drayton, *Memoirs,* I, 323; Barnwell, "Loyalism in S. C.," p. 100.

[34]Copy in SCHS *Collections,* II, 72-73.

[35]Drayton, *Memoirs,* I, 323. Campbell was handicapped by distance and being a newcomer to the colony, but their connection with the Governor gave Fletchall, Robert Cunningham and Joseph Robinson prestige. According to Landrum *(Col. and Revol. Hist.,* p. 44), the Loyalists sent around "well-paid emissaries" who distracted the minds of the Back Country people who had not yet been there many years and who saw the Association as "intended only to dragoon them into submission."

[36]Dabney and Dargan, *Drayton,* p. 93.

[37]Fletchall to Council, July 24, 1775, in Gibbes, *Doc. Hist.,* I, 123-24.

[38]The order was dated June 26; text of it in Jour. of Cou. of Safety, in SCHS *Collections,* II, 29. The small militia garrison at Fort Charlotte was to be invited to join the Provincial militia. Dabney and Dargan, *Drayton,* p. 92, call this the first military action of the Revolutionary War in South Carolina.

[39]Apparently with Kirkland's knowledge, his men had already deserted at Ninety Six and gone off to the muster. Barnwell, "Loyalism in S. C.," p. 103. Thomas Brown was irked at the timidity of Fletchall, who he recalled desired the bolder souls "to take such measures as to us appeared most practicable but with a Resolution on his part not to afford us directly or indirectly any Assistance." James H. O'Donnell (ed.), "A Loyalist View of the Drayton-Tennent-Hart Mission to the Upcountry," in *S. C. Hist. Magazine,* LXVII (January, 1966), 20; hereinafter cited as O'Donnell, "Loyalist View." Basically this is a long letter of Thomas Brown's written later that year.

[40]Barnwell, "Loyalism in S. C.," pp. 101-02.

[41]Many Loyalists were late arrivals who had never taken root.

[42]Barnwell, "Loyalism in S. C.," p. 113; Olson, "Loyalists and the Amer. Revol.," 201-02; Dabney and Dargan, *Drayton,* pp. 90-91. Writers disagree as to whether he was English or Scotch-Irish.

Chapter III
Search for Cohesion by Persuasion

At the very time that the general muster on the Enoree was casting a shadow over the prospects for the revolutionary movement, and while backwoods militants were joining the less militant neutralists, the Council of Safety was laying strategy to win over the anti-Charlestown men of the Up Country. To achieve this miracle, the revolutionary party decided to send out spokesmen "to make a progress into the back country, to explain to the people the causes of the present disputes, between Great Britain and the American Colonies." Representing the Council of Safety, William Henry Drayton and the Reverend William Tennent were designated as "commissioners" for this awesome task which took on the appearances of both a bush-whacking expedition and the antic-filled "stump speakings" which later were to typify South Carolina politics.[1] To give added clout to these itinerant spokesmen, they were armed with a commission directing "all the friends of the liberties of America" to "afford them every necessary aid, assistance and protection" as they went forth "to explain . . . the unhappy public disputes" and "to settle all political disputes between the people — *to quiet their minds,* and to enforce the necessity of a general union in order to preserve themselves and their children from slavery."[2] As if that were not enough sufficient in itself, the Council of Safety directed the militia and rangers "to furnish such assistance, support, and protection" as might be necessary.[3]

Thus was launched in July what historians usually refer to as the "Tennent-Drayton mission," somewhat of a misnomer since three other colonial leaders also were authorized to participate as official spokesmen: the Reverend Oliver Hart, Colonel Richard Richardson and Joseph Kershaw.[4] At times the whole group was together; at other times, they separated and meandered around on different fronts. Some spent longer at this task of "quieting the minds" of the people than did others.

It was a shrewdly chosen group for the task. An earlier mission consisting of George Wagner and Felix Long had been sent out to charm the German element but had accomplished nothing.[5]

Despite his early support of England, there was no question of the dedication now of William Henry Drayton to the revolutionary cause. He was perhaps radical enough in his thinking to have decided by then that secession from England was desirable. Impulsive though he was, he was wise enough to know that political reality would have prevented his saying so. Few dared yet to say they favored outright independence; even the first "state" constitution in March 1776 would be labeled only a temporary expedient to guide matters until there was a "return to normalcy." Drayton's dedication to the cause now seemed sufficiently intense that it must have stemmed from deeper feelings than resentment at his being pushed aside earlier by placemen from two government appointments.[6] By 1774, he was writing to deny Parliament's right to legislate for America and was advocating a North American parliament, not unlike Galloway's Plan of Union proposed to the Continental Congress a few months later. Serving on all major revolutionary councils, he had become steadily more aggressive in 1775.[7]

As a Calvinist minister and already a dedicated spokesman for the revolutionary party, William Tennent was well chosen to go to "explain . . . the causes of the present disputes" to the Scotch-Irish. His family had migrated from Ireland between 1716 and 1718 and distinguished themselves in the ministry. His grandfather founded the "Log College" in Pennsylvania to educate Presbyterian ministers; his father was one of the founders of the College of New Jersey, later Princeton, from which William Tennent graduated. In 1772, he came to Charlestown as minister of the Independent Church.[8] In 1774, he began speaking out on political issues and publishing anonymous letters to Charleston newspapers. He sat in the first Provincial Congress in June 1775 and served on the committee which drew up the Association.[9] Described by a modern scholar as "one of the new southern preachers who gave evidence of systematic propaganda activity," he began agitating for the radical party after 1773. It was said that he rarely involved politics in his sermons, but he "frequently spoke on Sundays at the court-

William Henry Drayton (1742-1779) was the firebrand of the Revolutionary movement in South Carolina. He had earlier become a Council member
but later adopted a radical course. As president of the Provincial Congress,
he advocated strong measures that headed toward war.

house and is said to have done a great deal of writing for the press."[10]

The third traveler was also an influential preacher calculated to achieve more rapport with the Back Country than might a Low Country planter or Anglican rector. The two major formative forces on early Baptist history in the state were Richard Furman and Oliver Hart. When Hart came from Pennsylvania to become pastor of the Baptist Church in Charlestown in 1750, "The Baptist cause immediately felt the uplift of a new and powerful personality...."[11] The next year he organized four churches into the second Baptist association in America, one that served as a model for others. He also attracted that other pillar of Baptism, Richard Furman, into the "Regular Baptist" fold when he was eighteen; the two remained close friends for life. Not only could he communicate in the Baptist meeting houses but "with an ecumenical spirit that was advanced even for the 18th century" he could easily make contact with all Dissenters.[12]

The other two commissioners were influential, successful Back Country settlers themselves, both living east of the Catawba-Wateree. Joseph Kershaw had migrated from Charlestown in 1758 and started a store at Pine Tree Hill, which ultimately became the important town of Camden. Richard Richardson had come from Virginia, settled along the Wateree and developed a huge estate called Big Home Plantation. Besides being a magistrate, he was a delegate to the Commons House representing St. Mark's Parish — that gigantic Back Country precinct.[13] He was also colonel of the militia regiment east of the Broad, and thereby as influential as any individual in the area. Both he and Kershaw had been elected to the First Provinical Congress from St. Mark's and were helpful in the 1775 mission because of their knowledge of the men and conditions in the region.

The main objective of the commissioners was to get signatures to the Association; their main target was the militia.

On August 2, 1775, the "progress to the back country" began for the gentlemen seeking to explain "the unhappy public disputes" and "to quiet their minds." Their primary job was "to discuss and persuade, not to fight."[14] It was an arduous, delicate task that involved not only political dangers but personal hardships that often appear in the diaries and memoirs that three of them left for readers many generations later.[15]

Such a venture was arduous even for people of that day. Traveling together, Drayton and Tennent left Charlestown at 6 a.m. on

The Association

"The actual commencement of hostilities against this continent, by the British troops, in the bloody scene on the 19th of April last, near Boston—the increase of arbitrary impositions from a wicked and despotic ministry—and the dread of instigated insurrections in the colonies—are causes sufficient to drive an oppressed people to the use of arms: We therefore, the subscribers, inhabitants of South-Carolina, holding ourselves bound, by that most sacred of all obligations, the duty of good citizens towards an injured country, and thoroughly convinced, that, under our present distressed circumstances, we shall be justified before God and man, in resisting force by force; DO UNITE ourselves, under every tie of religion and of honour, and associate, as a band in her defence, against every foe: Hereby solemnly engaging that, whenever our Continental or Provincial Councils shall decree it necessary, we will go forth, and be ready to sacrifice our lives and fortunes to secure her freedom and safety. This obligation to continue in full force until a reconciliation shall take place between Great-Britain and America, upon constitutional principles—an Event which we most ardently desire. And we will hold all those persons inimical to the liberty of the colonies, who shall refuse to subscribe this association."

From the Journal of the Provincial Congress

Revolutionaries submitted an "Association" to citizens all over the colony for their signatures in an effort to pressure them "to stand up and be counted." A major objective of the Tennent-Drayton mission was the solicitation and affirmation of Back Country support.

August 2 in a chaise and spent the night at Thomas Broughton's —
now Mulberry Plantation on the Cooper — having covered about
thirty miles (modern road distance). The only event that Tennent
found worth recording in his diary was their meeting forty Catawba
Indians on the way to town.[16] The second night was "spent no-ways
agreeably, owing to the noise of a maniac, occasionally there." The
next night was hardly better: "I had a sick and sleepless night, owing
to some green corn eaten at McG—s."[17] (Moderns complain over
such tragedies as poorly adjusted air conditioners in motels.) By
the evening of August 5, they had covered the one hundred thirty
miles that brought them into the area called "the Congarees" — on
the south side of the Congaree River across from and a bit below
modern Columbia.[18] Here they stayed with Colonel John Chesnut.[19]

Around the Congaree Store[20] the whole traveling party now
converged. Colonel Richardson arrived August 6 to go on "the
Errand,"[21] and Colonel Joseph Kershaw was there by August 7.[22]

The travelers lingered in the Congaree area for several days. The
German element here was among the least disposed to support
the radical cause, partially because they were convinced that opposition to the King would lose them their land grants.[23] In general, the "German Loyalism was inclined to be passive, and hence
not dangerous to the Revolutionary cause."[24] The Germans —
or "Dutch" — had heard by this time a rumor that the commissioners would unleash the Rangers on them unless they signed
the Association. In order to "take off the fears of the people," the
Rangers in the area were disbanded for a few days.[25] At the same
time, however, the German settlers were subjected to some pressure
or duress: "to excite the private interests of the Dutchmen," word
was passed that the non-subscribers (to the Association) would not
be able to purchase at, or sell to, the Congaree Store or to Charlestown.[26] Economic warfare and crucial embargoes are not new.

On August 6, two companies of militia were mustered and the first
of many efforts to sway a crowd politically was launched. As
Tennent depicted the scene, "Mr. Drayton harangued them and was
followed by myself; until all seemed satisfied. . . ."[27] It must have
been like a revival since "the falling tears from the audience showed
that their hearts were penetrated, and that we might hope for
success." All but fifteen of the audience signed the Association.[28]
Later that same night there was a mutiny in the militia camp; the
trouble blew over by the next day, Drayton blaming "three or four

privates of profligate characters" and Tennent blaming "some words dropped by some officers concerning their pay and tents."[29]

On August 8, Drayton and Tennent crossed the Congaree to attend an election (just north of the site of present Columbia). Despite the frustration they had met at the Congarees, their frequent and verbose reports back to their sponsors, the Council of Safety, reflect optimism and report success, for "despite some evil disposed persons" who sought to "do mischief," they claimed that they "had the good fortune to speak so as to be universally understood," and even the outside "troublemakers" wisely "became converts and cheerfully signed the Association." In addition, new volunteer companies of militia loyal to the Congress were being formed.[30] Such campaigning may not have seemed normal to a Low Country gentleman, but Drayton did not complain — although his friend Arthur Middleton consolingly wrote him, "I am sorry to hear you have been under a necessity of exercising your abilities upon the soldiery by sermons and harangues — I wish that you may not have thrown your jewels among swine."[31]

Concluding their mission in the Congaree area, the commissioners paused in their "harangues" and sent a lengthy report to headquarters and expressed satisfaction with their errand and outlined their plans for the future.[32] While there, they had learned that Moses Kirkland, militia captain-turned-Loyalist, had been to Charlestown to see Governor Campbell and would return "full freighted from his Excellency, with commissions, papers, and offers of encouragement, to Colonel Fletchall; and . . . to all the malcontents, in the upper parts," all of which would undoubtedly do much "to poison the minds of the people — and . . . to defeat the objects of the Commissioners."[33] Irritated, the said commissioners suggested that they might "apprehend" Kirkland and send him to Charlestown, and urged that the Council then not treat him leniently.[34] Obviously he was not one of the people whose minds they planned to "ease." Brinkmanship became a possibility, as did deterrant action.

Planning for all of them to rendezvous again at Colonel Fletchall's home on Fairforest (in present Union County), the apostles of the radical party set forth on their various itineraries as they moved out from the Congarees. Oliver Hart, the Baptist minister, left on August 8, went up the Saluda and crossed into the Dutch Fork which he found to be a "fine country" of "high Land & good water." He was always delighted when he found "a good Baptist

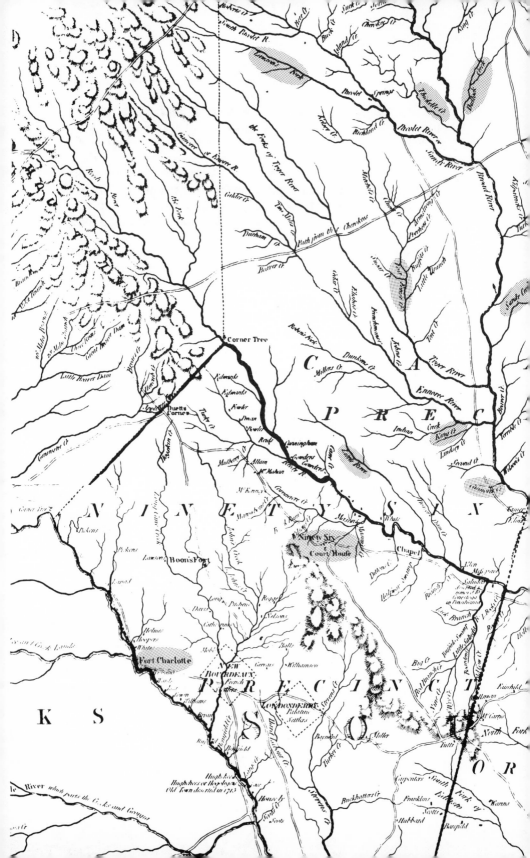

Map from the collection of South Caroliniana Library

A detailed section of Henry Mouzon's 1775 map of North and South Carolina includes many of the sites visited by the Tennent-Drayton mission of 1775.

family" and was willing to preach on request at services or meetings hurriedly arranged: "I took occasion to speak on the State of national affairs, they heard with Attention, and I was told one opposer was convinced and sharply reproved one who quarrel'd with the Sermon."[35] Staying west of the Broad, Hart crossed the Enoree and Tyger rivers, arriving in the Fairforest[36] area where he stayed with another prominent Baptist minister, the Reverend Philip Mulkey.[37] Hart must have been quite disconcerted by his brother preacher since he found that he "rather sides with ministerial Measures, and is agt those adopted by the Country. Altho he professes Himself difficulted about these Things; The People, in general, are certainly (as they say) for the King; . . . one Man, with whom we conversed, fairly trembled through Madness."[38]

Hart was discouraged at the people "so fixed on the Side of the Ministry, that no agreement on the Country side seemed to have any Weight with them; they generally acknowledge that they know little about the Matter, and yet are fixed . . . . "[39] A fellow Baptist, the Reverend Joseph Reese, abetted Hart's efforts, but the people were "extremely obstinate"; indeed, "one of them wish'd 1000 Bostonians might be kill'd in Battle — One wish'd there was not a grain of Salt in any of the sea Coast Towns on the Continent."[40] Colonel Fletchall, who lived in the area, attended a service on August 12 when Reese preached. Opposition was encountered and the tables turned on August 14 when at a meeting called by Mulkey (Hart's host in the area) Major Joseph Robinson read an "Address to the People of America," a document presenting the ministerial side of the controversy and one which was to plague the Back Country mission more later. "With Sorrow I saw Marks of approbation set on every Countenance," lamented Hart, who concluded that "Col. Fletchall has all those people at his back."[41]

In this depressed mood, the Reverend Hart went to join the other commissioners at the nearby home of Colonel Fletchall.

While Baptist Hart had been on that excursion, Presbyterian Tennent had been carrying the message to the other side of the Broad into the Camden judicial circuit. Accompanied by Colonel Richardson, Tennent preached at Jackson's Creek Meeting House.[42] He too encountered closed ears: "After sermon harangued the people an hour on the state of the country, some of the most sensible were the most refractory I had met with, obstinately fixed against the proceedings of the Colony."[43] Still, Tennent was usually optimistic — or whistling in the dark. On August 13, although he apologized for "the subject of my mission on the Lord's day, harangued at large [at Rocky Creek Meeting House];[44] was supported by Col. Richardson. The heat almost melted me; but had the pleasure to see all the people eagerly sign the Association fully convinced of the need of it."

Tennent constantly complained of the ardors of travel. His Sabbath success "haranguing" once lost its luster for him that night:

> Rode ten miles in the evening through the rain to Captain_____, if we can stand this, we need fear nothing; but the imclemency of the skies was not to be compared to the fury of the little inhabitants of the bed. After a sleepless and wet night, I was shocked by the blood and slaughter of my calicoed shirt and sheets in the morning.[45]

He, too, encountered the effectiveness of the royal "Address to the People of America" ("it is at present their Gospel"), and was especially frustrated because the people of the "back parts" had been taught "that no man from Charlestown can speak the truth, and that all the papers are full of lies."[46] Thus, as early as the eighteenth century there were those who distrusted both "outside agitators" and the media.[47]

Meanwhile the "big gun" of the Back Country mission, Drayton, had been proceeding through the Dutch Fork toward the Fairforest meeting, being accompanied by Kershaw. Going about ten miles up the south bank of the Saluda, he was confounded by the "Dutch sensibilities" and, hence, unloosed again his threat of economic coercion — that no miller who was a subscriber to the Association should grind wheat or corn for non-subscribers and, hence, he said, his auditors were "brought more to reason."[48] The next day (August 12), he crossed over the Saluda into the Fork and went to Evan McLaurin's Store where he "did not procure one subscriber. McLaurin threw a damp upon the people, as did some other leaders whose names I have taken down."[49]

Drayton was particularly downcast by John Adam Summer, who was successfully opposing him in the Fork, and he decided to skip a Sunday (August 13) service where he had been scheduled to speak, since he preferred to "save myself the mortification of preaching to a people who were obstinate and would not hear." Kershaw and Drayton therefore departed from "that stiff necked generation" and moved on to King's Creek, a tributary of the Enoree River in present Newberry County.[50]

There, however, the storm of opposition that he confronted was even greater — and took on a new twist on August 15. Having completed a successful speech to the gathering, Drayton learned that Robert Cunningham, one of the stronger-minded and more aggressive Loyalists from the Saluda valley, had arrived and wanted to speak also — or, as South Carolina politicians later were to put it, to "divide time." Thus, at King's Creek came about South Carolina's first real "stump meeting" with two leaders from opposing parties or factions debating the issues before a crowd. The two opponents then had dinner together, but Drayton recalled that he "spoke to him [Cunningham] seriously and politely, but all was in vain."[51] While at King's Creek, Thomas Brown — that most formidable Loyalist who had arrived with Cunningham — read the crowd Sir John Dalrymple's Address from the People of England to the People of America,[52] the same document which Hart and Tennent had been encountering. This address sought to show that they were embarked on a truly precarious course: the British controlled the sea, and slaves might revolt during a civil war. The address was calculated to make one pause: It also warned that British military force was powerful, that closing of trade would wreck the colonies and that the outstanding differences could easily be settled. One statement of the address probably struck a responsive chord in the Back Country: "It is hard that the charge of our intending to enslave you should come oftenest from the mouths of those lawyers who in your southern provinces at least, have long made you slaves to themselves."[53]

After Brown's reading, Drayton, according to his own report, "answered the whole. I applied ridicule . . . , the people laughed heartily and Cunningham and Brown could not but grin — horribly." Drayton reported those present as saying "Cunningham was beaten off the field," and "highly mortified, he and his worthy companion of tar and feather memory, stole away."[54]

After "the stump meeting" at King's Creek, the leaders of both factions now moved to Colonel Fletchall's Fairforest home for a genuine "summit conference."[55] Perhaps Fletchall and the commissioners hoped for a detente. They might have established such with the Colonel — described by Tennent as "the great and mighty nabob, Fletchall" — but they found him "surrounded by his court, viz. [Robert] Cunningham, [Thomas] Brown, and [Joseph] Robinson; who watch all his actions, and have him under great command."[56] The Low Country-Up Country abrasion was still starkly evident: "We soon found the unchangeable malignity of their minds and . . . bitterness against the gentlemen as they are called. . . . [They] believe no man that comes from below. . . ."[57]

Photo by Sam Hilborn from *Battleground of Freedom—South Carolina in the Revolution*, copyright 1970 by Sandlapper Press, Inc.

The pre-Revolutionary road to Charleston passed through Ninety Six. Remains of the old village are located beyond the stile to the right.

Instead of a detente, the summit conference was turning out to be a confrontation with Cunningham presenting a bristling obstacle to the itinerant missionaries for revolution. He was not a resident of Colonel Fletchall's regiment area but lived on land on the Saluda River near the present Newberry-Laurens county line. A native of Pennsylvania, he had moved to South Carolina and settled in the Saluda valley where he was a magistrate and a captain in the regular militia. He was described as "a man of great popularity." According to our best authority, his loyalism stemmed from resentment against the Low Country — maybe because he lost his post as magistrate for participating in the Regulator Movement. He also became irked at the Provincial Congress when it was distributing commissions in its new Provincial militia.[58]

To get around the "hard-liners" who surrounded Fletchall, "the gentlemen" talked to that worthy separately for three hours after breakfast. Drayton said that they tried to instill confidence in the Colonel; perhaps they meant backbone (which, however, is rarely planted by flattery) because both sides were increasingly coming to discover his indecisiveness.[59] Maybe they should not have expected too much activity and hustle from Fletchall since he was described as being "very corpulent," weighing over two hundred eighty pounds, and being over fifty years old and hardly able to travel.

Born in 1757, Fletchall was in South Carolina by 1757 (early for the Back Country). He owned 1,665 acres, had at least fourteen slaves, had designed a mill and held positions as magistrate, coroner and colonel. His wife was the sister of Ambrose Mills, the most important Loyalist in western North Carolina. Maybe he was under the influence of an in-law, but certainly he seemed to be much under the influence of Cunningham and Robinson.[60]

Drayton described their confrontation:

> We endeavored to explain every thing to him. . . . We endeavored to show him that we had confidence in him. We humored him. We laughed with him. Then we recurred to argument . . . to join his countrymen and all America. All that we could get from him was this. He would never take up arms against the King, or his countrymen; and that the proceedings of the Congress at Philadelphia were impolitic, desrespectful, and irritating to the King.[61]

They charged him with having been in touch with Governor Campbell, which he did not deny. The Drayton implication was that there was something heinous in such correspondence, with Fletchall seeing nothing particularly unique or reprehensible about one's having contact with one's legally appointed chief executive — one then in a line of succession one hundred five years old. Such different attitudes underscore the tragedy of the impasse that was an American Revolution — here, conflicting men, citizens of the same colony, under English Kings for generations, both presumably sincere, both patriotic about their native land and about the proper object of their loyalty. With greater patience on both sides, with fewer hotheads, with less selfishness and more willingness to see the other view, with greater statesmanship and understanding in London, the tragedy need not have flowed on to bloody schism, secession and war. Perhaps in due season — even in the late eighteenth century — a "British Commonwealth of Nations" or a "British Common Market" might have been feasible. Obviously, such a happy resolution of the problems was not inevitable; but neither was the Revolutionary War inevitable, even when it was beginning to erupt at many places — including the banks of Fairforest Creek.

The Low Country travelers marked the "malignity" of those surrounding Fletchall because they "misled people who are ignorant." Here at the Fairforest summit meeting, Drayton and Tennent began to size them up: Cunningham — "The man's looks are utterly against him; much venom appears in Cunningham's countenance and conversation"; Brown — "the spokesman; . . . his bitterness and violence, is intolerable."[62] Thomas Brown did say much that was provocative, and a fight between him and Drayton was averted only when Fletchall sent the former to bed. The radicals did get one promise from the Colonel — much to the annoyance of his lieutenants: that they would all gather together again a week later for another general muster of the regiment and an election to be held at John Ford's on the Enoree River. Presumably this would give the itinerant evangelists a chance to present the view of the Council of Safety to the rank and file of the regiment.[63] Here was another chance for a stump meeting and for swaying the mind of the frontiersmen.

The commissioners on their "errand" again dispersed after the Fairforest meeting, agreeing to gather on August 23 at Ford's. Richardson and Kershaw left the others at this point and returned to their homes east of the Wateree. Tennent also headed off eastward toward the Camden District and continued to be thwarted by assemblies which, despite his harangues, refused to sign the Association, in his judgment a "refusal which proceeded from the grossest ignorance and prejudice."[64] After going to the New Acquisition area (present York), he headed south to Bullock's Creek and then west again to the Thicketty area (between modern Spartanburg and Gaffney) where "I mounted the pulpit and spoke near two hours." Despite the presence of Major Robinson's friends, "the people seemed convinced, and after my writing an Association from memory, refreshed myself, and drank out of a cow bell." Those gathered "signed the association and retired, seemed contented." Confident in his power of persuasion, two days later he headed for the muster on the Enoree.

After the Fairforest conclave, the Reverend Hart had headed west into the Lawson's Fork area (modern Spartanburg). On August 21 he joined up with Drayton there at Captain Joseph Wofford's.[65] Latter-day South Carolina politics also was previewed: "A beef was barbecued, on which all dined."[66]

Drayton had come to the Lawson's Fork region much shaken by the strength of the opposition. To cope with it, he began organizing there new units of rangers who would be at Fletchall's rear. He also learned of rumors of an impending attack on Fort Charlotte and started machinery for reinforcing the fort. More alarming were rumors of Indian touble; hence, Drayton sent word to the Cherokees by Richard Pearis to get six of their leaders to meet him at Amelia (below the Congarees) in twelve days for talks.

The only ray of bright light seemed to be the attitude of the people around Lawson's Fork who were quickly and enthusiastically joining the new volunteer militia that was loyal to the Provincial Congress. It was being organized here into a new regiment being formed under Colonel John Thomas, Sr., and called the Spartan Regiment[67], a faction somewhat unique in the midst of so many King's Men.

In a long letter to the Council of Safety, Drayton showed that his own thinking and planning were beginning to clarify and take on a new direction. Despite the commissioners' optimism at first, their errand had not really won over the Piedmont and the "detente" at the Fairforest "summit" had certainly not resolved matters. As for the next scheduled meeting at Ford's, "I do not expect any success; I apprehend some insults."[68]

Drayton then proposed to the Council that when he arrived later at the Amelia area camp of Colonel William Thomson (commander of the Rangers in the Orangeburg District), he remain there "till I see every spark of insurrection extinguished." The way to accomplish this: take the offensive and prevent the Loyalist leaders — he suggested a dozen — from being at large. If they were "secured," he predicted "a commotion" would follow but that without leaders — and especially Kirkland — the Loyalist faction would decline.[69] To use modern terminology, he was proposing a "pre-emptive strike."

In that mood, Drayton headed for the all-important meeting at John Ford's on the Enoree.[70] The Reverend Tennent arrived, as did the Reverend Hart and his traveling partner, the Reverend Joseph Reese. Even more of the Loyalists coverged on the meeting where both Drayton and Tennent had predicted trouble and perhaps violence: Colonel Fletchall, Captain Robert Cunningham, Thomas Brown, Major Joseph Robinson, and Moses Kirkland himself, who had just been to Charlestown to confer with Governor Campbell. Instead of a thousand militiamen to whom Drayton and Tennent had hoped they could make an appeal, only two hundred fifty showed up.

The conclave took on overtones of another "stump meeting" with both sides forced to "divide time." Fletchall's associates were fearful of his proclivity for what today would be called "neutralism," with Thomas Brown alarmed that the Colonel "was more interested in retaining his good standing with the revolutionary leaders of Charleston than in providing positive leadership for the loyalist party."[71] When the militia men were gathered "to hear what was to be said in publick affairs,"[72] Drayton "began to harangue them, and was answered in a most scurrilous manner by Kirkland . . . , and a terrible riot seemed on the point of happening."[73] The threatened bloodshed was averted, but the Council of Safety received this description from their commissioners of the speeches by Kirkland and Brown: "Imagine every indecency of language, every misrepresentation, every ungenerous, and unjust charge against the American politics, that could alarm the people, and give them an evil impression of our designs. . . ."[74] Even the missionaries from Charlestown admitted they had failed, winning few if any adherents of this latest "stump meeting" which may have been one of the most crucial and important in South Carolina history. No leaders had budged, but Drayton now was more determined than ever that the Provincial Congress would never have any chance of achieving control of South Carolina until and unless the Loyalist leaders were subdued — or locked up.

From this confrontation on the Enoree, Drayton started on a new and dangerous task — to liquidate Loyalist leaders.

His associates from the pulpit continued the "speaking tour" aspects of the Drayton-Tennent mission. They had had some success between the Broad and Catawba, and more in the Lawson's Fork area; but with the Germans and with areas between the Broad and Saluda, they could claim little. Now they turned south of the Enoree, and once they reached the region between the Saluda and Savannah, they had mixed results.[75] Their harangues found some willing to listen.

Hart and Reese moved to Duncan's Creek (in modern Laurens County) and spent several days using their Baptist friends as contacts. Once the elders of the Presbyterian Meeting House (on Duncan's Creek) brought themselves to approve, they preached here also and then parted.[76] Hart proceeded on to the Little River Meeting House (Presbyterian, in modern Newberry County near the Laurens line). Meeting him there was Tennent, who immodestly thought it "providential that we came here, as some opposers had collected who would have browbeat Mr. Hart; took the storm upon myself, and did some good."[77] From here Hart crossed the "Saludy" and went down its south bank back to Chesnut's place at Congaree, where it had all started.[78]

Like Hart, Tennent had also left Ford's muster place and gone into the present Laurens County where he spent much time with James Williams on Little River,[79] preaching two and a half hours to a group in the middle of Robert Cunningham's Loyalist area. Although he crossed the Saluda several times, he spent most of this time south of it — plagued repeatedly by rains, discomfort and high water at fords and ferries. A modern traveler should read Tennent's diary: "rode thirty-six miles, part in the rain; slept upon a broken clay floor all wet, and the wind and damp blowing upon me; passed a bad night."[80] While visiting the Long Cane Creek area (of modern Abbeville), he stayed with Patrick Calhoun, father of John C. Calhoun. At Bull Town Meeting House, about fifteen miles from the Indian line, he was most satisfied with his performance:

> Preached extempore with more ease and freedom than common. The people though mostly opposers, appeared very affectionate. Finding them willing to hear, I gave them a discourse . . . of near three hours; I think I was more animated and demonstrative than usual. Its effect was very visible, the people holding a profound silence for more than a minute after I was done.

After three hours, it may have been possible they were asleep.

Tennent waxed eloquent about the richness and the economic potential of the Savannah River valley. After a visit to Fort

Charlotte on the river, he moved down to Augusta. He left that area on September 8 en route to Charlestown, where he arrived on September 15 after a trip generally close to the river.[83]

Since leaving Ford's on the Enoree, Drayton — the real leader of the "errand" — was less involved with speaking to audiences and with trying to win coverts or to "ease the minds of the people." Discouraged by the failure at persuasion, Drayton was turning to more direct action and militant tactics. He now was considering a resort to force.

Footnotes To Chap. 3

[1]Minutes of Council of Safety, July 23, 1775, in Gibbes, *Doc. Hist.*, I, 105-06; also in SCHS *Collections*, II, 58.

[2]*Ibid.*, in Gibbes, *Doc. Hist.*, p. 106; emphasis by this writer.

[3]A separate order of July 23, in *ibid.*

[4]Drayton, *Memoirs*, I, 324.

[5]Dabney and Dargan, *Drayton*, p. 91; McCrady, *S. C. in Revol., 1775-80*, p. 34.

[6]Positions as assistant judge and as member of the Council.

[7]*Dictionary of American Biography*, V, 448-49.

[8]Theologically broad — Presbyterian, Congregationalist and Independent. It is the forerunner of the present Congregational Church. Early called a meeting house, it is the source of the name of Meeting Street.

[9]See Newton B. Jones (ed.), "Writings of the Reverend William Tennent, 1740-1777," in *S. C. Hist. Magazine*, LXI (July, 1960), 129-33. Also, see MS sketch of Tennent by Robert W. Weir, in Tennent Papers, South Caroliniana Library.

[10]Philip Davidson, *Propaganda and the American Revolution, 1763-1783* (Chapel Hill: University of North Carolina Press, 1941), p. 25.

[11]Loulie Latimer Owens, *Saints of Clay: The Shaping of South Carolina Baptists* (Columbia: South Carolina Baptist Convention, 1971), p. 35. For a sketch of Hart, see this useful book, chap. 5.

[12]*Ibid.*, p. 37. Hart was also an opponent of slavery and fervently wrote the wish "that all Bigotry was rooted out of the earth. . . ."

[13]He was also the founder of a dynasty. One son and a grandson became governors. A daughter married a Manning. Six governors have been named either Manning or Richardson — all related. Wallace, *History*, III, 70. On his home, see *Names in South Carolina*, XV, 34.

[14]Anne King Gregorie, *History of Sumter County* (Sumter: Library Board of Sumter County, 1954), pp. 9, 24, 25, 39, 65; Thomas J. Kirkland and Robert M. Kennedy, *Historic Camden* (2 vols.; Columbia: The State Company, 1905), I, *passim*.

[15]Dabney and Dargan, *Drayton*, p. 95; Drayton, *Memoirs*, I, 324. The Drayton account is the one cited so frequently here, *Memoirs*. The Hart Diary is in the South Caroliniana Library in its original manuscript; it will soon be edited and published by Loulie Latimer Owens, who kindly advised us about it and permitted our use of her transcript — a double kindness since after about ten days on his trip the rascal started writing in cipher! It is not too difficult to break his secret, but it is much easier to have Mrs. Owens' translation. The Tennent Diary is available in three places: a manuscript copy (early but not the original) in the South Caroliniana Library; a printed version of that one in Gibbes, *Doc. Hist.*, I, 225-39; and another printed version, slightly different, in the *Charleston Year Book*, 1894, pp. 295-312. Citations herein are to the Gibbes version, since it is more available, having been reprinted in 1972 by The Reprint Company. By internal evidence, one has to correct his dates since he "didn't know what day it was" from August 14 to August 25. (In the manuscript, he has the day of the week; Gibbes omitted that.) Drayton's *Memoirs*, I, chaps. 8 and 9, are in effect Drayton's diary of the trip.

[16]Tennent Diary, August 2, in Gibbes, *Doc. Hist.*, I, 225.

[17]*Ibid.*, August 4, in *ibid.*, I, 226.

[18]Various settlements have existed in the area near the point where the Congaree Creek flows into the Congaree River. Above this confluence, on the south side of the Congaree, the early river town of Granby appeared. Indian paths also had converged on this area.

[19]Chesnut was elected to the Provincial Congress for the District between the Broad and the Saluda, and was elected paymaster for the Regiment of Rangers. *Jour. Prov. Cong.*, pp. 6, 49.

[20]"Congaree Store" was "just below the large ditch, which crossed the road [old State Road?] a few hundred yards below Granby." Explanatory footnote in Gibbes, *Doc. Hist.*, I, 124.

[21]Oliver Hart Diary, August 6, 1775, in South Caroliniana Library. On August 7, Hart met Drayton and Tennent at Chesnut's. From Hart's Diary, it appears that Chesnut's house was south of the Congaree. Coming from Charlestown, he had stopped also with a Colonel Thomason, who must have been William T. Thomson who lived in present Orangeburg County and headed the Rangers.

[22]Drayton to Council of Safety, August 7, 1775, in Gibbes, *Doc. Hist.*, I, 130.

[23]Drayton, *Memoirs*, I, 325.

[24]Barnwell, "Loyalism in S. C.," p. 94.

[25]Tennent Diary, August 5, in Gibbes, *Doc. Hist.*, I, 226.

26Drayton, *Memoirs*, I, 326. In the presence of some of the German leaders, Drayton wrote to the Council of Safety requesting them to guard the town gate and ask for certificates from all wagoners to show that they had joined the Association. Landrum, *Col. and Revol. Hist.*, p. 47. Evidently the Council had earlier approved such pressure; see Drayton to Council, August 9, 1775, in Gibbes, *Doc. Hist.*, I, 135.

27Tennent Diary, August 6, in Gibbes, *Doc. Hist.*, I, 226. Hart did not arrive there till the next day. Points made by Drayton in his speech are summarized in a report to the Council, August 7, 1775, in Gibbes, *Doc. Hist.*, I, 129-30.

28Drayton to Council, August 9, 1775, in Gibbes, *Doc. Hist.*, I, 134.

29Drayton, *Memoirs*, I, 328; Tennent Diary, August 7, in Gibbes, *Doc. Hist.*, I, 226.

30Drayton to Council, August 9, 1775, in Gibbes, *Doc. Hist.*, I, 134.

31Arthur Middleton to Drayton, August 11, 1775, in Gibbes, *Doc. Hist.*, I, 136.

32Drayton and Tennent to Council, August 7, 1775, in Gibbes, *Doc Hist.*, I, 128, 133.

33Drayton, *Memoirs*, I, 330.

34Drayton and Tennent to Council, August 7, 1775, in Gibbes, *Doc. Hist.*, I, 133.

35Hart Diary, August 9, 1775.

36The Fairforest Church, one of the oldest Baptist congregations, was between Fairforest Creek and the Tyger in modern Union County.

37On Mulkey and the Fairforest Church, see Joe M. King, *History of South Carolina Baptists* (Columbia: South Carolina Baptist Convention, 1964), pp. 71-72.

38Hart Diary, August 10, 1775.

39Hart Diary, August 11, 1775. Hart may have been confronting the kind of obstacle described to this writer by a modern minister: "If they arrived at their position by means other than reason, it just does not do much good to waste time trying to reason with them."

40Hart Diary, August 11, 1775. Joseph Reese had an important career in the Baptist ministry, being influential in the founding of the High Hills of the Santee Church which has had such a impact on Baptist history. See King, *Hist. of S. C. Baptists*, pp. 80 and *passim*.

41Hart Diary, August 14, 1775.

42Jackson's Creek runs southwest of modern Winnsboro.

43Tennent Diary, August 11, 1775, in Gibbes, *Doc. Hist.*, I, 227.

44Rocky Creek enters the Catawba from the northwest in the area of modern Great Falls in southeastern Chester County. He had also sent word ahead to the people along Fishing Creek. He apparently had been trying to contact some of Colonel Neel's regiment quartered near Mr. Tim's tavern on Sandy River, which is in modern Chester County southwest of the town of Chester.

45Tennent Diary, August 13, 1775, in Gibbes, *Doc. Hist.*, I. 228.

46*Ibid.*, August 14, 1775, in *ibid.*, I, 228.

47The Charlestown papers were supporting the American cause against the Ministry.

48Drayton, *Memoirs*, I, 362. His discourse on August 11 to a "Dutch Church" had not won a single subscriber. Drayton to Council, August 16, 1775, in Gibbes, *Doc. Hist.*, I, 141. Apparently Drayton's *Memoirs* were largely written on the basis of these dispatches that went to Charlestown leaders.

49Drayton to Council, August 16, 1775, in Gibbes, *Doc. Hist.*, I, 141.

50Summer had signed the Association in Charlestown but now was described as "a false brother." Drayton also blamed "a few influential, and in general illiterate persons." Drayton, *Memoirs*, I, 364; Drayton to Council, August 16, 1775, in Gibbes, *Doc. Hist.*, I, 141. Evidently he was moving in a northwesterly direction, coming from the Saluda River and heading toward Kennedy's Ford on the Enoree, in the area of present Whitmire. King's Creek was described as about ten miles below Hendrix' Mill on the Enoree and about 180 miles from Charlestown. Drayton described it as if the whole settlement stretched about ten miles up to Hendrix' Mill. This is on the south bank of Enoree, downstream a bit from modern Whitmire. See the endpiece map in Pope, *History of Newberry*, I; also copies of the James Cook map (1773) and the Henry Mouzon map (1775) help those with good eyes. Also, see the John Wilson map (1822).

51Drayton to Council, August 16, 1775, in Gibbes, *Doc. Hist.*, I, 142.

52*Ibid.* John Dalrymple was a Scottish lawyer in Lord North's ministry. The radicals kept expressing horror at the fact that the Address had been supplied to Brown by Governor Campbell.

53Olson, "Loyalists and the Amer. Revol.," p. 210.

54Drayton to Council, August 16, 1775, in Gibbes, *Doc. Hist.*, I, 142. Also, see Drayton, *Memoirs*, I, 367; Landrum, *Col. and Revol. Hist.*, pp. 47-48. One can wish for an observation from the other side. Nearly all of the descriptions available come from radical participants. Excellent antidote to this is the article already cited, Olson, "Loyalists and the Ameri. Revol.," built around Thomas Brown. There is also the Loyalist assessment of affairs contained in a lengthy letter from Brown to Governor Campbell, October 18, 1775, in James H. O'Donnell, "A Loyalist View," previously cited.

55Fletchall's home, Fairforest, was located on the creek of that name about five miles southwest of the present town of Union. Landrum says that it was later known as the Murphy Mill Place, and then was a part of the McBetts estate. After the Revolution, Fletchall left the country and went to the West Indies; his estate was confiscated and taken over by a Colonel Brandon. The Brandon place is labeled on the John Wilson map of South Carolina (1822). Also, see Landrum, *Col. and Revol. Hist.*, p. 48.

56Moses Kirkland was absent, being in Charlestown at the time. Joseph Robinson lived on Broad River in Camden District, and was a major in the militia of Colonel Thomas Neel's regiment of the "New Acquisition" area. Olson, "Loyalists and the Amer. Revol.," p. 205. Neel was in the "regular" militia but, like Richardson, had become loyal to the Provincial Congress. See *Jour. Prov. Cong.*, p. 102. Also on Robinson, see below pp. 76-77.

57Tennent to Council, August 20, 1775, in Gibbes, *Doc. Hist.*, I, 145.

58Perhaps somebody "ought to make a study" of how often "Tory" and "Patriot" support stemmed from annoyance over rank and reward. Somewhat like a college's honorary degree, for every friend made, several enemies are made. On Cunningham, see Barnwell, "Loyalism in S. C.," pp. 97-98. Robert Cunningham had two brothers, Patrick and John. The infamous "Bloody Bill" Cunningham, who won his unenviable sobriquet and earned his reputation about 1781, was a cousin.

For information more voluminous than objective, see "Civil Warfare in the Carolinas and Georgia," in *Southern Literary Messenger,* XII (1846), 321-36; 385-400; 513-24; 577-86, a review article of Samuel Curwen's *Journal and Writings.*

[59]The whole session at Fletchall's home lasted over twenty-four hours, beginning on the morning of August 17.

[60]Barnwell, "Loyalism in S. C.," pp. 94-95; Olson, "Loyalists and the Amer. Revol.," pp. 204-05, 211-12.

[61]Drayton to Council, August 21, 1775, in Gibbes, *Doc. Hist.,* I, 150.

[62]These are Drayton's terms. See Gibbes, *Doc.Hist.,* I, 150.

[63]Eyewitness accounts of the August 17-18 "summit" at Fairforest: Tennent to Henry Laurens August 20, 1775, in *ibid.,* I, 149-51; Drayton, *Memoirs,* I, 368-69, 410-11; Hart Diary, August 17, 1775.

[64]Tennent apparently went north and northwest from Fairforest. On August 19, he refers to King's Creek which appears to be the one near modern Blacksburg — not the one earlier visited on the Enoree. He spent that night with "Col. Polk," apparently Colonel Ezekiel Polk, member of the Provincial Congress from the New Acquisition. The next day (Sunday, August 20) he preached at Barsheba Meeting House and traveled on to Bullock's Creek.

[65]Joseph Wofford was a brother of Benjamin Wofford, a Loyalist with Fletchall, and was the father of another Benjamin Wofford, who was to be the founder of Wofford College. For more on the group, see David Duncan Wallace, *History of Wofford College* (Nashville: Vanderbilt University Press, 1951), pp. 18-19.

[66]Hart Diary, August 21. He arrived at John Ford's on August 23.

[67]Thus originated the later names of "Spartan District" and then Spartanburg. The militia was inspired to its "Spartan" name by the ancient Greek military group. Despite some rather extravagant optimism in the travelers' letters, this success in the Spartanburg area was the first real enthusiasm they seemed to have met among the settlers.

[68]Drayton to Council, August 21, 1775, in Gibbes, *Doc. Hist.,* I, 153.

[69]*Ibid.* He asked for clear orders and authority on this subject, and observed that without such action, all of their efforts would have been in vain.

[70]Landrum, *Col. and Revol. Hist.,* p. 53, says that the old muster ground lay between Cedar Shoals Creek and the Enoree, "at or near the old Davis Newman place."

[71]Olson, "Loyalists and the Amer. Revol.," pp. 211-12.

[72]Hart Diary, August 23, 1775.

[73]Tennent Diary, August 23, 1775, in Gibbes, *Doc. Hist.,* I, 230. On this trip, Drayton always carried a dirk and a pair of pocket pistols. The Cunninghams were said to have "appeared here with arms, sword and pistol." Drayton, *Memoirs,* I, 378, 379.

[74]Drayton and Tennent to Council, August 24, 1775, in Gibbes, *Doc. Hist.,* I, 157.

[75]Barnwell, "Loyalism in S. C.," pp. 108, 109; Tennent Diary, *passim.*

[76]Reese had also been to Warrior Creek (present Laurens County) to speak.

[77]Tennent Diary, August 29, 1775, in Gibbes, *Doc. Hist.,* I, 232. Tennent seems to have been much more of a fire-eater than was Hart, especially if one can judge from the topics and tenor of their diaries.

[78]Muchly condensed from Hart Diary, August 23-September 4, 1775.

[79]There are many Little Rivers in South Carolina. This one rises in Laurens County, flows through Newberry and empties into the Saluda.

[80]Tennent Diary, August 30, 1775, in Gibbes, *Doc. Hist.,* I, 232. The wife of Major James Mayson was drowned crossing a swollen creek while she was returning from a sermon. *Ibid.,* August 27, in *Ibid.,* 231.

[81]Tennent Diary, September 2, 1775, in Gibbes, *Doc. Hist.,* I, 233. On September 1 when he reached the Rocky River at Bull Town, west of the modern town of Abbeville, Tennent was at the westernmost point that any of the commissioners on this 1775 odyssey reached.

[82]He gave several interesting descriptions of the little town and a rather detailed one of Fort Charlotte.

[83]Tennent's diary is particularly detailed about the period of August 27-September 15, when he tells more of what he saw and less of his harangues and their success. Generally he was making more success with his cause than he had earlier. He occasionally noted that the inhabitants were living in great terror of the Indians — a result of the "Governor's intrigue." Drayton praised Tennent's work, "diffusing political and moral information with that zeal and address, which ... marked his conduct throughout the progress of the Commissioners." Drayton, *Memoirs,* I, 382. After he left Augusta, he stayed on the Georgia side of the river until he crossed over into South Carolina at Two Sisters Ferry, from whence he headed for Charleston.

Chapter Four
Search for Cohesion by Coercion

Since South Carolina has well been called "the battleground for freedom," obviously many of the persons who constituted the apparent majority in the summer of 1775 must either have subsequently changed opinions or have been dragooned into silence. Of course, maybe many who resented the Low Country revolutionaries should not be considered to have been so much actively royalist as quietly passive, for the loud sounds were coming not from them but from Thomas Brown, Moses Kirkland and other aggressive King's Men. Actually, one should be wary of the estimates, statistics and claims as propounded by both sides.

Although the Drayton-Tennent mission failed to convert the Back Country to the plutocratic radicalism of the Provincial Congress, South Carolina nevertheless later was to become much more anti-British. (The writer keeps deliberately avoiding the traditional term and saying they became "Patriots.") There seem to be two reasons for the decline of Loyalism from its peak of July 1775: (1) the militant policy of William Henry Drayton which the radicals pursued between August 1775 and the end of the year, a policy which won over some Loyalists and kept the neutralists passive; (2) the blunders made later by inept English politicians and military men in the field. Notable in South Carolina was to be the tendency of soldiers like Patrick Ferguson and Banastre Tarleton. During 1780-82, both active and potential Loyalists were virtually driven into the radical camp.

But our concern for the moment is the policy that Drayton pursued once the "errand into the Back Country" had failed to "quiet the people's minds."

After the disconcerting confrontation at Fletchall's muster at Ford's on August 23, Drayton crossed the Enoree and headed south and by August 27 was at the little Back Country court seat, Ninety Six. Arguments having been inadequate, Drayton was now determined to crush the Loyalist party by resorting to force. Convinced that most of the opposition came simply from backwoodsmen who disliked the Charlestown leadership but were unconcerned about the ruckus with the mother country, Drayton felt that their threat to the radical movement could be defused if only the leaders were subdued. He also knew that though they were noisy and probably numerous, they were neither united in aims nor driven by enthusiasm.[1] Even so, he had to be careful and cautious since his own radicals might well shrink back if he should trigger a full-out collision that would only harden the opposition. The most radical of the Charlestown groups, the Council of Safety, wrote him at the end of August that they "viewed with horror the spectacle of a civil war." Uneasy about their man in the field, within two weeks they issued another caveat to him because of his bold brinkmanship.[2]

After raising some more volunteer troops in the Ninety Six area, Drayton went to Snow Hill, Captain Leroy Hammond's place opposite Augusta, only to learn of a plan[3] for the King's Men, under the leadership of Moses Kirkland, to attack Fort Charlotte and seize the arms and supplies so badly needed by their side. Seeing this as an opportunity to rid the radical leadership in the Charleston area of Kirkland and his leadership of Back Country royalists once and for all, Drayton took the offensive. On August 30, he reported to the Council of Safety that he was taking vigorous military action to forestall an effort to seize the fort or to stifle the attack if it should be attempted. Moving like a major military commander in his theater of operations, he ordered Major Andrew Williamson to move men to Harlen's Ford (about thirty miles upriver from Augusta); ordered Colonel William Thomson of the Rangers to post three hundred men along the Ridge;[4] and ordered Colonel Richard Richardson to move three hundred men near the confluence of the Enoree and Broad rivers, these being in a position to threaten Fletchall's militia if they should move in support of Kirkland. To justify his actions, Drayton cited as authority an August 11 letter to him from the Council.[5] In this war of nerves, he also issued the same day a proclamation declaring that Moses Kirkland was seeking "to violate the public peace" and proclaiming that any who assisted him would be "deemed public enemies to be suppressed by the sword."[6]

The show of force made by Drayton and his militiamen seemed effective since the coup plotted against Fort Charlotte never took place. Later, Thomas Brown said that "Drayton's Band of Ruffians" need never have been gathered, the whole commotion having been but a "pretense of suppressing a Body of Men raised by Colonel Kirkland," which actually consisted only "of 4 men whom Colonel Kirkland kept about his Person to prevent his being butchered by Drayton's Orders."[7] According to Drayton, however, his strategy had worked most effectively, and as for Kirkland, Drayton claimed he had "paralized his exertions" and thus caused him to drop his plans.[8] Kirkland sent his brother with an offer of surrender in exchange for a pardon, but the radical leader refused, demanding unconditional surrender. After that, Kirkland "lurked about for some days" with Drayton's forces in search of him. According to Brown, about twelve bushwhackers were seeking to capture Kirkland, Cunningham, and himself, the pursuing forces being "composed of the most notorious Horse thieves in this Province, men desperate thro extreme Poverty to which their crimes had reduced them & ready for hire to execute the most Atrocious Designs." Brown indelicately suggested that they were "fit Instruments" for such "detestable villainous Purposes."[9]

After the commotion which left the more radical Loyalists "continually on the Wing," Moses Kirkland escaped the trap and headed for Charlestown where the Governor gave him asylum on a British ship. There the remarkable frontiersman convinced His Excellency that he had a plan which could reduce the Southern colonies if the British would send equipment and a few officers to support the 4,000 men he could recruit, and therefore he was sent on to Boston to lay his plan before General Thomas Gage. En route, his ship was taken just before reaching Boston and he was imprisoned.[10]

With Kirkland disposed of, Drayton and some of his new recruits moved from the Savannah River area back to Ninety Six near the Saluda and indulged in a crafty game.[11] Aware of the division within the opposing force but knowing that neither side had an overwhelming superiority, Drayton "marched to the brink" in a show in which he hoped the other man "would blink first" without any shots being fired. It was a dangerous ploy.

Drayton's scheme was to make a bid for neutralism — to try to get a commitment for it from the potentially dangerous majority while making threats against them — as if he were driving them to the carrot with a stick. As one of his enemies bitterly described it, "Having fixed his Head Quarters at Ninety Six he detached Parties with orders to rifle houses break locks and seize the papers of those who had opposed the Designs of Congress. These Parties I believe acquitted themselves to his satisfaction having stolen Horses and destroyed Corn . . . ." Drayton suspected that Robert Cunningham and Thomas Brown were collecting men, and "the malcontents" of Fletchall's area were reputedly gathering at O'Neall's mill (north of the Saluda) on September 10 preparatory to an attack on Ninety Six, about ten miles south of them. The not-very-aggressive-or-dashing Fletchall himself came into the area with two hundred fifty men and, as Thomas Brown petulantly noted, "As Colonel of that District we resigned the Command to him — his presence foreboded no good . . . ."[12] It was a smouldering situation. The Loyalists probably had more men but were hesitant. Apparently both sides wanted to avoid a full-scale collision. Meanwhile, Colonel William Thomson and his rangers and Major Andrew Williamson and his foot soldiers had joined Drayton at Ninety Six in this grand military checkers match.

Drayton divided his forces, placing some in the fortified gaol at Ninety Six, some at Island Ford on the Saluda under Major Mayson, and the bulk in a defense position halfway in between. In his not-very-modest account later to the Council of Safety, Drayton said that he had to restrain his people from an attack since many lives would be lost. He also introduced a bold ruse into the proceedings: He sent to Colonel Richardson, north of the Broad, a message designed to be intercepted by the Loyalists and directing him to move on their Saluda force from the rear, and saying that he had also sent orders to Colonel John Thomas (in the Lawson's Fork area) "to burn the houses & destroy the Plantations of all the Non-subscribing absentees."[13] Drayton calculated that the numbers of his enemy would "ebb and diminish," particularly since they were "under no command."[14]

During this "Sitzkrieg," Drayton on September 13 sent word to those north of the river that they would not be harmed if they signed the Association and went home peacefully.[15] The tone of the document sounded a note of reasonableness to all but the "hard-liners" — with the goal "to prevent the effusion of civil bloodshed." As always, the radicals told the Loyalists that the "hellish scheme" stemmed from "an abandoned administration" that was deceiving the King, and from "men of low degree among us" who were "knowingly deceiving their neighbors." Many of the former Regulators may have had their antipathy to Low Country planters tempered when Drayton assured them that they — who had never been deeply involved in the trans-Atlantic row — had nothing to fear from the Council of Safety if only they would go home and "choose to behave peacefully," for, after all, "We shudder even at the idea of distressing them, in any shape; we abhor the idea of compelling any person to associate with us . . . ."[16]

Now fully into his war of nerves, Drayton invited the Loyalist leaders to come to his camp for reasonable negotiations.[17] As he must have anticipated, his invitation created consternation and deep wrangle in the Loyalist camp. Fletchall proved so weak and vacillating that his tough cohorts accused the "poor Dastard" of being so "struck with terror" that, according to Brown, he "went so far as to acquaint Drayton that it was his Opinion that we would submit to any terms."[18] If Thomas Brown is to be believed, when he (Brown) read Drayton's letter to their men,

> the People were raised to such a Pitch of Fury that it was with the utmost Difficulty we restrained them from attempting an attack in the Indian mode upon their Camp that very night which was at that time impracticable from the River Saluda's not being fordable.[19]

The "hawks" among the Loyalists proposed a strong reply to Drayton's pronunciamento:

> We must further observe we have as true & real Regard for Liberty established on constitutional Principles as any Men on the Continent by whatever name distinguished & shall take very proper legal Steps in our Power for its Preservation & Support.[20]

Fletchall rejected these belligerents in his camp and took with him six men described by Brown as being "as ignorant and illiterate as himself," "officers of inconsiderable Consequence as Messengers."[21] Cunningham and Brown drew up harsh "Instructions" and terms for their Loyalist negotiators to use, but they ignored them because, as Brown related it, Fletchall "distressed with Apprehensions in order to revive his spirits had such frequent Recourse to the Bottle as to soon render himself non compos — [and] whilst in such Condition Drayton . . . drew up the Articles."[22]

The "Treaty of Ninety Six" sounds complex if read in full, but simply put, it called for both sides to live and let live — in peace. The Loyalists agreed not to assist British troops, and Drayton pledged punishment to any Association man who molested a non-Associator. It was also agreed that one's failure to sign was not to be interpreted as an overt act of unfriendliness to the Provincial Congress. It granted to the Back Country the right to be neutralist.[23]

It was a very pragmatic solution, but not all involved liked it. It solved problems for Fletchall and the rank-and-file in the Dutch Fork, but it infuriated those who found "neutralism" unsatisfactory surrender and who, for varying reasons, abominated the gentlemen of the Council of Safety. Thomas Brown condemned Fletchall's "Timidity which he could not conceal from the People [and which] gave such general Offense that Captain Cunningham's men & mine insisted on having him drummed out of the Camp" but finally "with extreme Difficulty we moderated their Resentment against Fletchall."[24] Such was not general, for most of the till-now Loyalists went home satisfied with the civil peace that had been achieved. Presumably they were contemplating the prospect of sitting out the rest of the revolution.

Just as Brown did not think the peace a great accomplishment, so did some Charlestown gentlemen have misgivings. Only three weeks earlier the Council had been wavering about their man Drayton lest his impetuosity create too dangerous a crisis.[25] On August 31, the Council had granted him extensive powers, but his close friend, Arthur Middleton, had apprized him that the Council had a bare quorum present and the vote had been 4 to 3 — with expressions such as "creating a civil war — young man [Drayton was then thirty-three] — hot — rash — may raise the people, and set them to cutting one another's throats."[26] When the Council soon thereafter heard of his organizing troops to cope with Kirkland and the alleged threat to Fort Charlotte, they endorsed his new vigor, but also advised him to discharge the militia as soon as he could.[27] Now that he had negotiated a non-vindictive truce with the bulk of Loyalist forces, Henry Laurens feared that it would not serve its purpose saying that he regarded it as "a very bad and imperfect cure."[28]

Still disgusted, Thomas Brown headed for Charlestown, convinced that the Revolution would have ended in South Carolina if his harsh terms had been insisted on.[29] In town he tried unsuccessfully to see the Governor, whereupon the Council of Safety "with their customary Politeness took me into Custody & proceeded to interrogate me . . . ."[30] Because he insinuated that if "any Violence be offered to me" it would "be attended with the most fatal Conse-

Lithograph by Ole Erekson, 1876

Arthur Middleton (1742-1787) was a member of the Commons House of Assembly, later in the Provincial Congress and a member of the Council of Safety. One of the more extreme revolutionists, he was a close friend and neighbor of William Henry Drayton.

Henry Laurens (1724-1792), a planter and merchant, was a foremost Revolutionary statesman and served as president of the First Provincial Congress and of the Council of Safety. He also was a member and president of the Continental Congress.

quence in the Back Country," he was released — or so he explained it.[31] After a brief return to the Up Country, and following a warrant for his arrest, he fled to St. Augustine for safety.[32]

Drayton had virtually succeeded in his new tough strategy —"apprehending" or silencing the Loyalist leaders: Fletchall, never a strong leader, had been silenced by the grant of the right to be left alone; Kirkland had fled the colony and was soon to be captured at sea; Brown had fled and soon was to be in Florida. Only Robert Cunningham was still at large and a potential rallying point for dissidents.

Setting Cunningham up as a target, Drayton coped with him adroitly. Writing him a diffident, polite letter, he noted that he had heard that Cunningham refused to be bound by the new Treaty of Ninety Six, although "I am sincerely inclined to believe that these are not your sentiments."[33] Although basing his reasons on matters of principle, Cunningham walked into the trap by acknowledging that he would not be bound by it.[34] As a result, late in October he was seized by a party disguised as Indian traders acting on orders of the Council of Safety, accused of sedition and sent to Charlestown to be held incommunicado in a jail there.

With Cunningham gone, Drayton could now recite the later fable of the "Ten Little Indians" and smugly chant, "And then there were none." He did not. He said there was one more to get — and showed thereby he was not deeply sold on neutralism. The day after the Treaty, he had intoned these brimstonish words in a communication to the Council of Safety:

> But, after all, I assure you our safety is utterly precarious while the Governor is at liberty . . . . Gentlemen, allow me, in the strongest terms, to recommend that you make hostage of the Governor and the officers . . . . The Governor should be taken into custody.[36]

Even the radical Council had not reached that point.

On his way back to Charlestown, Drayton had one more duty to perform: to meet with Cherokee spokesmen and try to clarify their relations with the Congress and get from them commitments of peace and stability. For weeks there had been dark warnings of possible mischief afoot with the Cherokees, who were dissatisfied and hence susceptible to "evil men" who might seek to use them for their own purposes. Tennent kept hearing rumors of trouble, and just before the Treaty of Ninety Six Drayton was told that Brown and Cunningham were trying to stir the Indians to attack the frontier Associators.[37] Both John Stuart, then in East Florida, and Deputy

68

Superintendent Alexander Cameron, then with the Cherokees, were suspected and accused of inciting or planning to incite such mayhem. Apparently the suspicion was ill founded, but because of his jealously and the earlier personal vendetta with Stuart, Drayton could find it credible.[38]

In late September, Drayton headed out from Ninety Six to Congaree Store where he met Good Warrior and the Cherokee leaders who had been brought there by Richard Pearis.[39] Talking patronizingly to them, he explained the dispute between the English and the Americans (not very objectively, to be sure) and assured them of future economic support from the Provincial Congress, including a shipment of arms and ammunition which they badly wanted and needed. After he gave them presents, they went home "apparently satisfied."[40] Drayton then headed in the other direction — to the coast.

Just when Drayton was liquidating the Loyalist leadership, a new leader was being created by defection: Robert Pearis, who had accompanied the Cherokees. Born in Ireland about 1725, he had immigrated at the age of ten and had lived in Pennsylvania and Virginia before coming to South Carolina and settling on the headwaters of the Enoree and Reedy rivers. There he became prominent and influential among the Indians in the 1760s (he had one Indian wife) and was noted as an effective orator "of savage eloquence and power." At one time he claimed a tract of 150,000 acres, a mill (on the Reedy River in what is now downtown Greenville), a store, cattle and hundreds of acres in cultivation.[41]

After the Congaree meeting, Pearis switched sides and became a Loyalist — making the change as others in both factions had done, out of irritation over not being properly appreciated and rewarded, or so he thought. For bringing the Cherokees into contact with the Council, a meeting that should have led to harmonious relations, he expected to be rewarded with an appointment as Indian agent; instead, the post went to a rival. At the time, Pearis was deeply in debt to Charlestown merchants and needed money, and hence his switch to what was left of Loyalism.[42]

Both Drayton and Tennent now claimed more for their 1775 activity than was justified. They could return to the banks of the Cooper and say that the Back Country was now quiet. Better to have said it was passive, for these two had not been altogether suited by background or temperament to sway those people to become active partisans in behalf of the gentlemen of the Provincial Congress.

Those out in the woods were still not to be participating partisans until goaded by British mistakes and until led by men like Francis Marion, Thomas Sumter and Andrew Pickens.[43]

Drayton had eliminated the truly vigorous and committed Loyalist leaders. Still one more flare-up remained in 1775 before the civil turmoil was to end.

Chapter IV: Footnotes

[1]This awareness, of course, had not come to him suddenly.

[2]The first demurrer from the Council of Safety was dated August 31; a second was sent to him September 11. Drayton, *Memoirs,* I, 396-98.

[3]Tennent had first heard of the plan and notified Drayton of this possible attack which he said had been suggested by Governor Campbell. Tennent to Henry Laurens, August 20, 1775, in Drayton, *Memoirs,* I, 411-12.

[4]"The Ridge" northeast from Augusta, being formed between the headwaters of the Little Saluda and the forks of the Edisto. It is clearly visible in the James Cook map of 1773, as are many of the roads followed by these forces. Fort Charlotte was a post on the Savannah northwest of Augusta, opposite the mouth of the Broad River of Georgia. See also *S. C. Hist. Magazine,* LXVII, 20.

[5]Drayton to Council of Safety, August 30, 1775, in Gibbes, *Doc. Hist.,* I, 162-63.

[6]Gibbes, *Doc. Hist.,* I, 163-64. He also cited his commission of July 23 as authority.

[7]O'Donnell, "Loyalist View," p. 18. Whether the Kirkland plan against Fort Charlotte ever had really been seriously contemplated or actually launched seems a bit unclear, although certainly there were several predictions of it. Drayton had also learned that Kirkland was planning to disrupt a "meeting of the people" scheduled for September 1 at the Ridge.

[8]Drayton, *Memoirs,* I, 382.

[9]O'Donnell, "Loyalist View," p. 18.

[10]Olson, "Loyalists and the Amer. Revol.," p. 212. Also, see Moses Kirkland to Henry Laurens (from a Philadelphia jail), January 11, 1776, in Gibbes, *Doc. Hist.,* I, 254-55; also, in Edmund C. Burnett (ed.), *Letters of Members of the Continental Congress,* I, 191. This almost-illiterate letter is touching. Kirkland's career after his 1775 capture was long and exciting; see Barnwell, "Loyalism in S. C.," pp. 116-17; 372-75; 399.

[11]He left the Savannah on September 6 and arrived at Ninety Six on September 8, Drayton, *Memoirs,* I, 386.

[12]O'Donnell, "Loyalist View," p. 19. See map in Drayton, *Memoirs,* I, opposite 389. Drayton said that he had 1,000 men; Fletchall, 1,200. *Ibid.,* I, 389.

[13]O'Donnell, "Loyalist View," p. 21.

[14]Drayton to Council of Safety, September 17, 1775, in Gibbes, *Doc. Hist.,* I, p. 188.

[15]Brown said it was a sign of timidity on the part of Drayton when he discovered how strong the Loyalists were. O'Donnell, "Loyalist View," p. 20 Text of Declaration of September 13, 1775, in Gibbes, *Doc. Hist.,* I, 180-83. One cannot help but keep wondering how much the rank and file of the forces really understood such communications written to them in the ponderous, formal, stilted language of the educated aristocracy.

[16]Drayton, *Memoirs,* I, 393; also, Gibbes, *Doc. Hist.,* I, 182.

[17]Drayton to Council of Safety, September 11, 1775, in Gibbes, *Doc. Hist.,* I, 175.

[18]O'Donnell, "Loyalist View," p. 20.

[19]*Ibid.,* p. 21.

[20]*Ibid.,* pp. 21-22.

[21]John Ford, Benjamin Wofford, Thomas Greer, Evan McLaurin, Robert Merrick and the Rev. Philip Mulkey. Actually, four were captains of militia and Mulkey was the prominent Baptist preacher. McLaurin was the important merchant of the Dutch Fork.

[22]O'Donnell, "Loyalist View," p. 22. Brown also charged that while they were negotiating, some of Drayton's men "were committing their Customary Depredations upon the Property of our Friends." *Ibid.,* p. 23.

[23]Text of Treaty of Ninety Six, September 16, 1775, in Drayton, *Memoirs,* I, 399-403; also, Gibbes, *Doc. Hist.,* I, 184-87.

[24]O'Donnell, "Loyalist View," p. 19. McCrady also deemphasizes the importance of the treaty because Fletchall and his group had no authority to make it and because Cunningham and the "other principal men on that side" repudiated it. This was true, but who did have authority to speak for them? Also, the bulk of the group seemed to acquiesce in it. McCrady did note that it "allowed Drayton to retire with honor to the Board in town," and thus it maybe was another "peace with honor." McCrady, *S. C. in Revol., 1775-80,* pp. 51-52.

[25]Drayton claimed that he had a virtual blank check on the basis of the August 11 letter from the Council which said they were "perfectly satisfied that he would leave nothing undone, that should appear necessary." Drayton, *Memoirs,* I, 396.

[26]*Ibid.,* I, 396-97. The full Council had thirteen members.

[27]McCrady gives a lengthy analysis of the Council's reactions to the intensifying action. McCrady, *S. C. in Revol., 1775-80,* pp. 46-41.

[28]Henry Laurens to his son, September 26, 1775, in *S. C. Historical Magazine,* V. 79.

[29]Barnwell judiciously questions whether Brown — or all the Loyalists at the Saluda River confrontation — were in a position to make such demands. Barnwell, "Loyalism in S.C.," p. 121. Brown insisted that they were as opposed to bloodshed as was Drayton and "have as sincere Desire for Peace — as may restore Tranquility to this distracted Province." O'Donnell, "Loyalist View," p. 21; his terms, pp. 22-23.

[30]O'Donnell, "Loyalist View," p. 25.

[31]*Ibid.*

[32]*Ibid.,* p. 31. On Brown's later career, see O'Donnell, "Loyalist View," pp. 27-28; Barnwell, "Loyalism in S. C.," pp. 198, 336; Olson, "Loyalists and the Amer. Revol.," pp. 214-15. After the Revolution, he moved to the Bahamas where he died in 1825.

[33]Drayton to Robert Cunningham, September 21, 1775, in Gibbes, *Doc. Hist.,* I, 192.

[34]Cunningham to Drayton, October 5, 1775, in *ibid.,* I, 200.

[35]Olson, "Loyalists in the Amer. Revol.," p. 216. As will be seen, here was an example of the kind of folly that the English were later to commit: overreaching themselves when the tide was running in their favor. The calloused, high-handed treatment of Cunningham infuriated the now virtually leaderless Loyalist dissidents and inspired them to erupt again in a new uprising.

[36]Drayton to Council of Safety, Sept. 17, 1775, in Gibbes, *Doc. Hist.,* I, 189.

[37]Andrew McLean to Drayton, September 12, 1775, in *ibid.,* I, 176-77.

[38]See Drayton to Alexander Cameron, September 26, 1775, in Gibbes, *Doc. Hist.,* I, 194-95; Henry Laurens to Drayton, September 21, 1775, in *ibid.,* 192-93; Cameron to Drayton, September 16, 1775, in *ibid.,* 207-08. On earlier Drayton-Stuart troubles, see above, pp.

[39]Drayton met the five Cherokees on September 25 after they had been waiting several days to see him.

[40]Drayton, *Memoirs,* I, 407-08. For text of his speech to the Cherokees, see *ibid.,* I, 419-27. The colonials seemed to save their greatest bombast and verbosity for communications to Indians.

[41]Barnwell, "Loyalism in S. C.," pp. 122-23. Paris Mountain is named for this interesting personality.

[42]*Ibid.,* pp. 122-24.

[43]Dabney and Dargan, *Drayton,* pp. 105-06. Also, see Alexander Garden, *Anecdotes of the Revolutionary War, With Sketches of Character of Distinguished Persons* (Charleston: A. E. Miller, 1822; reprint: Spartanburg: The Reprint Co., 1972), p. 203.

Chapter Five
Winter Victory

Although the active opposition to the aggressive revolutionary faction seemed to have ended by mid-September, 1775, the first real fighting and bloodshed of the American Revolutionary War in South Carolina erupted that fall.

Momentous events transpired in Charlestown before the major action shifted again inland: On September 15, Provincial troops under the Council of Safety occupied Fort Johnson, which from James Island commanded the entrance to the harbor; in that same month, Governor Campbell dissolved the Commons House of Assembly; in addition, His Excellency departed his Meeting Street house in a town which he now found inhospitable and unsafe and took refuge on a British warship in the harbor. On November 1, the Second Provincial Congress convened for its first session. On November 11 and 12 came the first Carolina battle of the Revolution between the Provincial and royal ships in the harbor. The affair was of more significance historically than militarily: The colonists were trying to sink hulks in one channel to force traffic to sail under the guns of Fort Johnson. This battle was like one that began another war in the same harbor in 1861: It lasted two days and did not have a casualty on either side.[1]

Out of these events, "the radical plutocracy" emerged looking more secure while their pro-English opponents seemed to be steadily fading.

The Back Country continued to appear calm after the Treaty of Ninety Six on September 16. On the day that the Second Provincial Congress convened, November 1, it learned that Captain Robert Cunningham had been taken into custody and brought to Charlestown. Things were not so calm thereafter.

The formal charge against him was "high crimes and misdemeanours against the Liberties of this Colony." In his defense that he brought before the Congress, he pointed out that it was true that he did not feel bound by the Treaty of Ninety Six (not having signed it, and claiming that those who had did not have authority to do so), but that he "had since constantly behaved as peaceably as any man, — and although he had opinions, he had not expressed them but when asked." Nevertheless, he was committed to jail by a warrant signed by his old antagonist, William Henry Drayton, newly elected president of the Provincial Congress.[2]

Cunningham was popular and bold enough that his jailing was bound to have repercussions in the Up Country. Five days later, the Journal of the Provincial Congress recorded a new event: that Patrick Cunningham had seized the shipment of gun powder being sent by the Council of Safety to the Cherokee Indians.[3] Any involvement of the Indians into the division between the white settlers could add a flaming new dimension to the turmoil — just when the schism had been opened anew by Robert Cunningham's incarceration.

Patrick Cunningham's original plan had been to rescue his brother from the Charlestown jail. He had failed in that. If he had succeeded, the crisis probably would not have been as great as that which now exploded over a single wagonload of gunpowder. Here Indian relations were involved, an emotional issue at any time and especially so if it became a factor in the split just reopened among white colonists.

The militia loyal to the Provincial Congress instantly went into action to recapture the powder and lead. Major Andrew Williamson, who lived at Hard Labor Creek in Ninety Six District, activated his troops. Aware of the restlessness of the Cherokees recently because of the decline of supplies and aware of the everlasting phobia of frontiersmen about the possiblity of Indian raids, Williamson also sent a letter on Novermber 6 to Edward Wilkinson and Alexander Cameron, then in the Cherokee Nation, requesting that they tell the Indians of the shanghaied shipment and seek to keep them calm until a replacement shipment could arrive.[4]

All evidence indicates the truth of Williamson's statement and the sincerity of the Province leaders: The supplies being sent, in accord with the Drayton-Cherokee conference at the Congarees, had no nefarious purpose but were simply to maintain the considerable trade that had long existed between Charlestown and the Cherokees but which had been disrupted by the recent civil struggle within the colony.

But such was not the interpretation which those opponents of the Provincial Congress put on this arms traffic. To them it was mute evidence that the Charlestonians were arming the Cherokees so that *they* could fall on the Up Country settlers — those who had recently accepted neutralism but who still were not enthusiastic revolutionaries. It was probably easy for the leaders still at large to believe this charge or suspicion, and then to convince the typical backwoodsman of this latest evidence of the duplicity and inhumanity of the plutocratic rebels. Their logic was not as strong as their emotion. Nevertheless, the backwoodsmen praised Patrick Cunningham's seizure since the ammunition had been denied to the Indians and now could be used by the settlers in defense against the red men.

In their propaganda to stir up frontiersmen against the "irresponsible" Congress, the now-revived Loyalists utilized Richard Pearis, who had just recently switched to their side. His credibility was impressive since he was generally considered an "Indian expert" and since he had been at the meeting at the Congarees when Drayton met the Cherokees whom Pearis himself had brought there. He now gave an affidavit that the Council of Safety was actually providing the ammunition for an Indian attack on the Piedmont Loyalists.[5] Irked by thinking he had not been properly rewarded, here again was an example of a man's picking his side — or changing sides — out of pique or for purely personal reasons.[6]

Such propaganda as Pearis' affidavit had the desired effect as the Up Country flared up again. A lengthy "Declaration" of the Provincial Congress — sort of a government "White Paper" — sought to give the whole history of the Province's relations with the Indians and to give a convincing statement of their intent, warning that sending ammunition in the first place had been "the only probable means of preserving the frontiers from the inroads of the Indians." Unfortunately, "wicked men . . . have made many of their deluded followers believe, that this ammunition was sent to the Indians, with orders for them to fall upon the frontiers and to massacre the non-associators . . . ."[7] The most convincing point that the Congress statement made seemed to be that if the Indians were to fall on the frontiersmen as the Loyalists charged, how could they have been expected to be able to distinguish between

Photo courtesy South Caroliniana Library

Colonel Richard Richardson (1704-1780) was a Back Country planter and distinguished statesman who, despite his age, was leader of militia and spokesman for moderate tactics.

Associators and non-Associators? They probably all looked alike to an Indian.

Besides printing and distributing proclamations, a badly divided Congress was also taking more direct action against the Back Country whose settlers were now in flame: It was also authorizing a large call-up of the militia under Col. Richard Richardson (1) to "seize and to apprehend, the bodies of Patrick Cunningham" and six others who had taken the ammunition; (2) to recover "the ammunition feloniously and contemptuously taken"; and (3) to "do all such things as in your [Richardson's] opinion shall be necessary, effectually to suppress the present insurrection, and to intimidate all persons from attempting any insurrection in the future."[8]

Quickly both groups were assembling their forces. [9] The collision point again seemed to be Ninety Six, where Major Andrew Williamson was slowly gathering men. (Colonel Richardson, the top commander, was beginning far away on the other side of the Wateree.) Drayton at least kept his opposition informed of actions being taken and the rationale and position of the Congress, sending letters to Colonel Thomas Fletchall and others in the Saluda-Broad Fork.[10]

Andrew Williamson sat at Ninety Six, waiting on Colonel William Thomson and his Rangers from the Orangeburg area. By November 18, he had been joined by Major James Mayson and a small party, and they began fortifying themselves in a quickly built stockade. There were five hundred sixty-two men in this defending or Provincial force.[11]

By November 19, the "Insurgents" — or anti-Provincial Congress troops (or Loyalists, or whatever they should be called) — had swarmed into the area and laid siege to Ninety Six. Thus began the second battle of the Revolution in South Carolina and the first that involved bloodshed in that conflict. The attacking forces were said to number 1,892 men and were led by Major Joseph Robinson and Captain Patrick Cunningham.[12] In this group were Captain Richard Pearis and Evan McLaurin, the Dutch Fork storekeeper who perennially reappeared on the stage.

What ensued lasted three days and has been called the First Battle of Ninety Six. (The second came in May-June, 1781.) Some accounts are boringly lengthy, but detail seems unnecessary here.[13] In view of several recesses for negotiations, it seemed to have been a collision between two rather reluctant dragons. On November 22, 1775, a treaty — or really a vague but prolonged truce — was signed. One commentator described it as "the closest thing to a victory that the loyalists ever won in South Carolina,"[14] and he is perhaps also correct to judge that their willingness to withdraw shows the Loyalists' awareness of their weakness. The defenders were outnumbered and they too seemed just as willing for a truce since Colonel Richardson would not arrive in time to benefit them; more pressing was the then-unknown fact that they were almost out of powder, having only thirty pounds remaining of their original two thousand pound supply. One of the defenders was killed and several of the attackers in the three-day siege. The militia of Williamson also had had very little water until the third day when they completed digging a well forty feet deep. They were blessed with "thirty-eight barrels of flour with four live beeves in the fort."

The treaty provided for all prisoners to be released; the new fort was to be destroyed; the Loyalists were to retire north of the nearby Saluda River; a twenty-day truce was to be provided for public differences to be sent to the Charlestown headquarters of both sides; and any reinforcements were to be bound by the treaty and the cease-fire.[15]

The president of the Provincial Congress was correct to judge that it was "fortunately the end of an affair, which might have produced the most distressing consequences." The Loyalist "army" was made up of "very discordant materials" with "inferior leaders of the old insurgents." Colonel Fletchall was not there, but was said to have encouraged the siege — with his normal offer-to-hold-your-coat bravery. The attackers did not act very boldly, except those who managed to station themselves "at the brick gaol" where they alone "annoyed the troops under Williamson's command."[16]

The major consequence of the treaty was the separation of the belligerents with the Saluda as a temporary dividing line. Nothing came of both sides' reporting to their superiors in Charlestown. In a ridiculous wrangle, the Council of Safety caught and imprisoned the messenger from the Loyalists to the Governor.[17]

Even prior to the siege, Colonel Richard Richardson had been gathering militia under the broad terms of the order of the Provincial Congress. Interpreting his basic objective as being the "pacifying" of the Province, he had been heading for Colonel Fletchall's home territory when he deflected his course to head for the relief of Ninety Six. Being the superior officer of Williamson, Richardson did not consider himself bound by the Treaty of Ninety Six. So, when the siege was lifted by that agreement, he again changed course and now "marched upon those who, on the faith of the treaty, had disbanded their forces."[18] In short, his objective was much bigger than that of achieving a cease-fire at Ninety Six.

Richardson was gradually gathering an unusually large force for that era and was happily discovering that many in the Back Country were flocking to his command, a fact that perhaps indicates that Congress had been convincing in its denial of the charge that it had been arming the Indians to attack the settlers. Maybe even the Tennent-Drayton mission had been more effective than it had appeared at the time. Richardson had fifteen hundred men when he had crossed the Congaree en route to Ninety Six. He then swung back across the Saluda into the Dutch Fork with the objective of pacifying the area and mopping up any remnants of activist Loyalists. By December 2, he was encamped at Evan McLaurin's store, fifteen miles from the Saluda. Here his force began gathering size like a rolling snowball: Colonel John Thomas of the Spartan Regiment from Lawson's Fork appeared with two hundred men; Colonel Thomas Neel from the New Acquisition with another two hundred; Colonel Lyles[19] with one hundred fifty. With his own and Colonel Thomson's Rangers, he had about twenty-five hundred as he began the task of sweeping up the remaining Loyalists who had already lost their most vigorous leaders.

Discouraged and divided, the Loyalists in the Fork offered little resistance but were "hovering about" with never over four hundred "assembled in arms."[20] The same mood that had led to Drayton's leniency and compromise in the first Treaty of Ninety Six (September 16) surfaced again — the idea that leniency would bind non-Associators of the Back Country to the Provincial Congress more effectively than would conquest and oppression. On December 4, the Council wrote to Colonel Richardson suggesting that he ask "the Insurgents 'to lay down their arms' and to promise 'the strictest neutrality'; and thereupon to grant them 'terms of mercy, and protection'. . . ."[21] Even prior to receiving this directive, the Colonel had done virtually that on his own initiative on December 8.[22]

By December 12, Richardson had about three thousand men, some of whom had moved as far as Duncan's Creek. Increasingly leaders were surrendering or being captured, some "of the first magnitude," according to the Colonel. Among these were Colonel Thomas Fletchall and Captain Richard Pearis. Fletchall was "unkenneled" by some of Thomson's Rangers when they found him hiding in a large, hollow sycamore tree on Fairforest Creek.[23] From

Liberty Hill (on the Laurens-Newberry county line, six miles south of the Enoree), Richardson reported even more additions to his force but noted that the most determined of the King's Men still refused to submit. These bitter-enders had retreated into Indian country (west of the present Spartanburg, Laurens, and Abbeville counties) and were holed up at a camp at the Great Cane Brake on Reedy River in the southern part of present Greenville County (southwest of Fountain Inn). From there, under the redoubtable Patrick Cunningham, they were desperately seeking reinforcements from the Cherokees to the west (modern Pickens-Oconee area).[24]

To mop up this remaining cluster, Richardson detached thirteen hundred men who were at Hollingsworth's Mill about twenty-five miles away and sent them under Colonel Thomson "to break up this nest of sedition and turbulent spirits," as Landrum puts it with his usual absence of detachment.[25] Arriving on the night of December 21, the attackers waited till daylight to strike; their force was discovered when it had the Loyalist force almost surrounded on the morning of December 22. Cunningham shouted for every man to save himself, and he departed unceremoniously on a barebacked horse — bare even himself and without breeches, according to one chronicler.[26] Despite his escape, he was later captured and was sent for "commitment . . . to the common gaol in Charles-Town."[27] Colonel Thomson's restraint was credited by some for the fact that there was no great slaughter by the pursuing Rangers.[28] About one hundred and thirty prisoners were taken — the bulk of the force ensconced on the Reedy.[29]

With the collapse of this last redoubt, the forces of the Provincial Congress had cleared the colony of organized resistance. Richardson sent one hundred thirty prisoners to Charlestown, including practically all of the leaders and potential leaders — Fletchall, Pearis and others.[30] These, he averred, were the only ones "we thought proper to detain," they being "the most leading and active." As noted, Patrick Cunningham was to go later.[31]

The episode might be labeled "The Downfall of the Loyalists." It might also be called "The First Step in the Union of South Carolina" — a process which would take many generations to complete.

The return trip from the frontier was an epochal event for Richardson's force, which some say had come to number five thousand. The day after the Battle of the Great Cane Brake, snow began falling and came down for thirty hours, reaching a depth of two feet. As Richardson recalled:

80

Eight days we never set foot on the earth or had a place to lie down, till we had
spaded or grabbed away the snow, from which circumstance many are frost
bitten, some very badly; and on the third day, a heavy cold rain fell, together
with sleet. . . .[32]

Despite swollen creeks, the ill-prepared and poorly clothed army slowly moved and gradually dispersed to its different home areas, finally being dismantled at the Congarees. Thus ended the "Great Snow Campaign."

The hardships and ordeals endured here earned the admiration of many early historians. Such bravery and dedication undoubtedly do deserve approbation. Nevertheless, one might suggest that the wisdom and forbearance of the leaders was equally as effective in unifying the province under the "gentlemen." Maybe Richardson was not just engaging in wishful thinking when he observed "The People are now more convinced than ever of their being wrong." But he was dealing with something much more significant when he judged, "The lenitive measures have had a good effect . . . . On the reverse, had I burnt, plundered and destroyed and laid waste, seizing on private property, then thousands of women and children must have been left to perish — a thought shocking to humanity."[33] Maybe the mind of the colony was not as unified as he assumed, for the Back Country feeling against Charlestown was deep. But unity was to come definitely in due season, achieved by the British and especially by Tarleton, who had not learned the lesson which Richardson knew and was pointing up in 1775.

Maybe such prudent policy came from a sense of *noblesse oblige* which some of "the gentlemen" had. Maybe it was simple evidence that they *were* gentlemen and therefore concerned with humanity. Maybe it was sense — the common sense of learning from mistakes made earlier. But it was wisdom, and it was policy of the Congress as well as of Richardson. It is true that for their own time Richardson, Drayton and Henry Laurens were "radicals," relative "hardliners."[34] Nevertheless, they recognized the unwisdom of pushing their luck when they were in the driver's seat, of overreaching themselves when they had the strength to do so, of being calloused or arrogant when they were winning. They were a "radical plutocracy" all right and maybe were snobbish about their rough-and-rude fellow citizens away from "the city." They had belatedly come to realize that maybe such people were not all lovely but that they *did* matter. These frontiersmen did have reasons for their resentments about their problems, of their own "taxation without representation" within South Carolina, for example. But the Congress leaders were beginning to make changes and concessions — too slowly, perhaps, but steadily and even gracefully, in South Carolina's way. In 1776, for example, they began some correction of the inequity of representation.[35] Richardson was doing that in 1775: the "more lenitive measures." Maybe here lies the proof of leadership — one that can learn.

Thomas Brown, Moses Kirkland, Robert Cunningham and even Thomas Fletchall were not bad men. They "lost" in one sense. At one time, they apparently had an even larger following than did their opponents. They were a group described well by Professor D. D. Wallace:

> A spirited, suspicious people, animated by loyalty to their King, against whom in their remote homes they cherished no wrongs, resentful of unlawful attempts to control them, were convinced of the overwhelming power of the Provincial Congress, of the humanity of its officers and of the falsity of the charges that the Revolutionists planned to subject them to Indian massacre.[36]

They deserve the label "Patriots" too—because they were patriotic to the motherland under which all had been born, and quite as devoted to constitutional principles as they saw them as were their rivals.[37] Their "loss" was not entirely a matter of luck.

The victors, "the radical plutocracy" or the Revolutionists, maybe "won" because they were bigger men. Having some of the better qualities of gentlemen was an asset. Knowing how to conduct themselves when they were successful was part of it; unwise men can turn their own success into misery and tragedy for both themselves and others. Maybe they were learning that power does not have to corrupt. These leaders learned that — regardless of their manners, their poverty, their spelling — the hoi polloi of the frontier were a part of Carolina that had to be accepted and respected. Colonel Richardson did not want to be guilty of aught which might be "a thought shocking to humanity."

It is such dimensions that made some men of 1775 the Founding Fathers for South Carolina. Such dimensions still can be assets to leaders.

Chapter 5: Footnotes

[1]McCrady, *S. C. in Revol., 1775-80*, p. 73. Although considered outdated by some, McCrady still gives a good, coherent account. It is written from a Charleston view; events happening elsewhere are treated as mere sideshows.

[2]*Ibid.*, p. 86, Cunningham was not to have oral or written contact with any person whatsoever. *Jour. Prov. Cong.*, pp. 82, 83-84. Drayton may have felt that by this action they were eliminating the last vestige of Loyalist leadership in the province.

[3]*Jour. Prov. Cong.*, p. 99. About one thousand pounds of public gunpowder was hijacked, the incident taking place near Mine Creek, between the Ridge and Ninety Six, seventeen miles from the latter. Drayton, *Memoirs*, II, 64. The seizure was described in some detail in two affidavits; see *Jour. Prov. Cong.*, pp. 101-02.

[4]Text in Gibbes, *Doc. Hist.*, I, 209-10. Also, *cf.* Drayton, *Memoirs*, II, 65-66. Said he: "I am confident they [Indian head men] will be able to prevent this affair being productive of any breach of comity between them and this Province . . . ." Cameron was John Stuart's assistant.

[5]Olson, "Loyalists and the Amer. Revol.," p. 216.

[6]See above, chap. 4, page 68. Also, Drayton, *Memoirs*, II, 116. Drayton wrote Pearis as late as November 8, bringing him up to date on affairs and asking him to explain the situation to the Indians. Text in *Jour. Prov. Cong.*, p. 107.

[7]Text of Proclamation of November 19, 1775, in Gibbes, *Doc. His.*, I, 210-14; also, in *Jour. Prov. Cong.*, pp. 137-39. One is reminded of the American sale of arms in the Middle East in the 1970s.

[8]In Congress, November 8, 1775, *Jour. Prov. Cong.*, pp. 103-04. The conservative opposition to calling out Richardson's force was led by Rawlins Lowndes; the motion carried by 51 to 49. *Jour. Prov. Cong.*, p. 103.

[9]It is interesting (or ironic) that Drayton refers to those forces opposing the Provincial Congress (the revolutionaries) as "the Insurgents."

[10]Text in *Jour. Prov. Cong.*, pp. 106-07. Other addressees: John Ford, Thomas Green, Evan McLaurin and Benjamin Wofford.

[11]McCrady, *S. C. in Revol., 1775-80*, pp. 90-91.

[12]*Ibid.*, p. 91. Major Mayson said his enemies numbered 2,000. Gibbes, *Doc. Hist.*, I, 215. James Robinson (see chap. 3, n. 56) was born on the James River in Virginia and moved to South Carolina and settled on the Broad River in Camden District. In 1775 he was thirty-three years old and was a major in Colonel Neel's militia regiment of the New Acquisition. He had a modest amount of property and three slaves. Included in his property was a surprising number (for that day) of books, including some in Latin, Greek and Hebrew. He also had a taste for astronomy. After the Revolution, he held important positions in Price Edward Island, where he had settled. Barnwell, "Loyalism in S. C.," pp. 96-97.

[13]For description, see Drayton, *Memoirs*, II, 117-20; James Mayson to W. Thomson, November 24, 1775, in Gibbes, *Doc. Hist.*, I, 215-16; also, Andrew Williamson to Drayton, November 25, 1775, in *ibid.*, I, 216-19.

[14]Olson, "Loyalists and the Amer. Rev.," p. 216. Also, see Barnwell, "Loyalism in S. C.," p. 124; Drayton, *Memoirs*, II, 115-20; text, dated November 22, 1775, in Gibbes *Doc. Hist.*, I, 214-15; Drayton, *Memoirs*, II, 148-49.

[15]Barnwell, "Loyalism in S. C.," p. 124; McCrady, *S. C. in Revol., 1775-80*, p. 124; Drayton, *Memoirs*, II, 120. It might be called the Second Treaty of Ninety Six.

[16]Drayton, *Memoirs*, II, 121. McCrady leans very heavily on Drayton's accounts and viewpoints.

[17]Account of that imbroglio in McCrady, *S. C. in Revol., 1775-80*, pp. 93-94.

[18]McCrady, *S. C. in Revol., 1775-80*, p. 95.

[19]This group is difficult to identify. The name sometimes is spelled Lisle. There was a Lt. Col. John Lisle in Fletchall's Upper Saluda regiment. See McCrady, *S. C. in Revol., 1775-80*, pp. 11-15, 95; *Jour. Prov. Cong.*, pp. 76, 149, 181, 189.

[20]Drayton, *Memoirs*, II, 126.

[21]*Ibid.*

[22]Text of his declaration in *ibid.*, II, 126-27. In effect, the Congress party was offering to let the Back Countrymen be neutralists — again.

[23]McCrady, *S. C. in Revol., 1775-80*, p. 96; Landrum, *Col. and Revol. Hist.*, p. 76, with an inaccurate citation. Richardson to Henry Laurens, December 12, 1775, in Gibbes, *Doc. Hist.*, I, 240, says he was in a cave.

[24]Richardson was sending regular reports to Charlestown. See Gibbes, *Doc. Hist.*, I, 239-44; 246-53.

[25]Landrum, *Col. and Revol. Hist.*, p. 79.

²⁶Wallace, *History*, II, 147; McCrady, *S. C. in Revol., 1775-80,* p. 97; Richardson to Laurens, January 2, 1776, in Gibbes, *Doc. Hist.,* I, 246-67.

²⁷*Jour. Prov. Cong.,* p. 212.

²⁸McCrady, *S. C. in Revol., 1775-80.* p. 97.

²⁹Some said there were hardly more than that there; Drayton says there were 200. *Memoirs,* II, 132. Only one of the Provincials was wounded, and five or six of Cunningham's men were killed.

³⁰List in Gibbes, *Doc. Hist.,* I, 249-53.

³¹Neither Major Joseph Robinson, leader at the first Battle of Ninety Six, nor Evan McLaurin, the storekeeper, were captured. On February 6, 1776, they were still contained in a list of five important Loyalists still at large. *Jour. Prov. Cong.,* p. 176. Nearly all of the prisoners taken were soon released by the Council of Safety. Wallace, *History,* II, 148.

³²Richardson to Laurens, January 2, 1776, in Gibbes, *Doc. Hist.,* I, 247.

³³ *Ibid.,* p. 248.

³⁴"Radical" is maybe too broad a term, but it sets them apart from the "King's Men" who had not favored revolution. In early 1776, William Henry Drayton and Christopher Gadsden — not always in agreement — concurred with Tom Paine that the American choice lay between complete independence and slavery. Many other leaders among the "Radicals" were shocked by such thoughts from *Common Sense:* Henry Laurens thought the idea "indecent"; John Rutledge, treasonable. The first constitution for the state in March, 1776, was adopted to last only "until an accommodation of the unhappy differences between Great Britain and America can be obtained (an event which, though traduced and treated as rebels, we still earnestly desire . . . ." *Constitution of 1776,* in *Jour. Prov. Cong.,* p. 258.

³⁵"Resolved, That the district heretofore described between Broad and Saluda Rivers, be now divided into three, as well for the convenience of electors of members of Congress, as an account of the happy influence which it may have upon the peace and union of the inhabitants. . . ." The report, significantly, was made by the Rev. William H. Tennent, Minutes of Prov. Cong., February 9, 1776, in *Jour. Prov. Cong.,* pp. 182-83.

³⁶Wallace, *History,* II, 148.

³⁷After all, we still argue about the Constitution, and at least ours is all neatly written down in one place, whereas that of the English was not.

Other Books Available From The Sandlapper Store, Inc.

P.O. Box 841
Lexington, South Carolina 29072

BATTLEGROUND OF FREEDOM
South Carolina In The Revolution.
By Nat and Sam Hillborn. $20.00

FROM STOLNOY TO SPARTANBURG,
The Two Worlds of a Former Russian Princess.
By Marie Gagarine. $6.95

THE GREEN DRAGOON,
The Lives of Banastre Tarleton and Mary Robinson.
By Robert D. Bass. $6.95

LAUGH WITH THE JUDGE,
Humorous Anecdotes from a Career on the Bench.
By Bruce Littlejohn, Associate Justice,
The Supreme Court of South Carolina. $6.95

THE PENDLETON LEGACY,
An Illustrated History of the District.
By Beth Ann Klosky. $12.50

A PIECE OF THE FOX'S HIDE.
By Katharine Boling. $8.50

SANDLAPPER 1968,
A bound compilation of all articles from the 1968
monthly issues of "Sandlapper" Magazine. $20.00

THE SANDLAPPER COOKBOOK,
Compiled by Catha W. Reid and Joseph T. Bruce, Jr. $5.95

THE SOUTH CAROLINA DISPENSARY,
A Bottle Collector's Atlas and History of the System
By Phillip Kenneth Huggins. $12.50

DISPENSARY BOTTLE PRICING.
> Current prices of all known bottles as of Fall, 1971.
> Paperback. $1.00

SOUTH CAROLINA HISTORY ILLUSTRATED.
> Vol. I Nos. 1, 2, 4. each, $4.00

SOUTH CAROLINA: A SYNOPTIC HISTORY FOR LAYMEN
> By Lewis P. Jones. Paperback. $3.95

SOUTHERN FISH AND SEAFOOD COOKBOOK
> By Jan Wongrey $4.95

WHAT THE WIND FORGETS
A Woman's Heart Remembers.
> By Helen von Kolnitz Hyer
> Poet Laureate of South Carolina $7.95

WIND FROM THE MAIN
> A Novel by Anne Osborne. $6.95

CHILDREN'S BOOKS

ADVENTURES IN SOUTH CAROLINA,
An Educational Coloring Book.
> Written by Linda Hirschmann.
> Drawings by Sharon Applebaum. $1.75

LORD OF THE CONGAREE
Wade Hampton of South Carolina
> By William H. Willimon. $4.50

THE MYSTERY OF THE PIRATE'S TREASURE
> By Idella Bodie
> Illustrated by Louise Yancey. $3.95

THE NAME GAME,
From Oyster Point to Keowee.
> By Claude and Irene Neuffer.
> Illustrated by Bob and Faith Nance. $3.95

THE SECRET OF TELFAIR INN.
Written by Idella Bodie.
Illustrations by Louise Yancey. $3.95

SURGEON, TRADER, INDIAN CHIEF.
Henry Woodward of Carolina
By William O. Steele.
Illustrated by Hoyt Simmons. $4.50

TURNING THE WORLD UPSIDE DOWN
By William and Patricia Willimon. $4.95

THE WHANG DOODLE,
Folk Tales from the Carolinas.
Edited by Jean Cothran.
Illustrated by Nance Studio. $3.95

Prices subject to change.
Add 50c per book for mailing and handling.
S.C. residents add 4% sales tax to the cost of the books.